Guide

1

La
Cenerentola
(Cinderella)

Rossini

Anna Pollak (Tisbe) and Denis Dowling (Dandini) in the celebrated 1959 Sadler's Wells production (photo: Houston Rogers)

Preface

English National Opera Guides are intended to be companions to opera in performance. They contain articles and illustrations relevant to any production and not only those mounted by English National Opera. Of general interest, also, is the inclusion of the complete original libretto of the opera, side by side with an English translation. There are many reasons why sung words may not be clearly distinguishable, whatever the language and however excellent the performance. The composer may have set several lines of text together, for instance, or he may have demanded an orchestral sound through which no voice can clearly articulate. ENO Guides supply English readers with an opportunity to know a libretto in advance and so greatly increase their understanding and enjoyment of performances whether live, broadcast or recorded.

We hope the Guides will prove useful to new and experienced opera-lovers alike. An audience which knows what to look and listen for — one that demands a high standard of performance and recognises it when it is achieved — is our best support and, of course, an assurance for the future of opera in the English-speaking world.

Nicholas John
Editor

1

La Cenerentola
(Cinderella)

Gioachino Rossini

English National Opera Guides Series Editor:
Nicholas John

John Calder ● London
Riverrun Press ● New York

First published in Great Britain, 1980, by
John Calder (Publishers) Ltd., 18 Brewer Street,
London W1R 4AS
and
First published in the U.S.A., 1980, by
Riverrun Press Inc.,
175 Fifth Avenue,
New York, NY 10010

ISBN 0 7145 3819 1 paperback edition

BRITISH LIBRARY CATALOGUING DATA

Ferretti, Jacopo
    La cenerentola — (English National Opera guides; 1).
    1. Operas — Librettos
    I. Title   II. John, Nicholas   III. Jacobs, Arthur
    IV. Rossini, Gioachino Antonio   V. Series
    782.1'2   ML50.R835

Typeset in Plantin by Alan Sutton Publishing Limited, Gloucester.
Printed by Whitstable Litho Limited in Great Britain.

Contents

List of Illustrations

Fairy-tale and opera buffa: the genre of Rossini's 'La Cenerentola'

Philip Gossett

The *Cinderella* story exists in various guises among the folktales of people throughout the world. Its most characteristic version in the European tradition is that of Charles Perrault, published in his *Contes* of 1697 as *Cendrillon ou La petite pantoufle de verre (Cinderella or The little glass slipper)*. From Perrault derive the fairy godmother, the wicked step-mother, the Prince's ball, the midnight deadline, and the lost slipper, as well as the pumpkin, mice, rat, and lizards which become, respectively, the coach, horses, driver, and footmen, all indelibly associated with the story children still enjoy. Practically none of these elements, however, figure in the libretto by Giacomo Ferretti, *La Cenerentola, ossia La bontà in trionfo (Cinderella, or Goodness triumphant)*, set to music by Gioachino Rossini and first performed at the Teatro Valle of Rome on January 25, 1817. The absence of magical elements has frequently been ascribed to Rossini's presumptive dislike of supernatural events in opera and his consequent insistence that Ferretti avoid them. But this explanation rings false, for just ten months later the composer produced his *Armida* in Naples, with spectacular magical effects and scenic extravagance. To understand the genre of *La Cenerentola* and the particular way Rossini and Ferretti handle the story, we must examine the social milieu of operatic composition in early-nineteenth-century Italy, the actual literary sources of Ferretti's libretto, and a significant artistic trend in contemporary Italian operatic librettos: the emergence of the so-called 'mixed genre', *opera semiseria*.

The pressures under which a successful composer was expected to work in Italy during the first decades of the nineteenth century were staggering: three, four, or even five new operas a year were commonplace. Between October 1815 and the première of *La Cenerentola* in January 1817, Rossini, shuttling between Rome and Naples, mounted the first performances of no fewer than six operas: *Elisabetta, regina d'Inghilterra, Torvaldo e Dorliska, Il barbiere di Siviglia, La gazzetta, Otello,* and *La Cenerentola*. The well-documented case of *Il barbiere* is notorious. A month before its first performance, Rossini began to receive the poetry from his librettist, Cesare Sterbini. A month before the première of *La Cenerentola* the subject had barely been chosen. Nor did the composer really have a month to work. Orchestral parts had to be copied, singers had to learn their roles by memory, and the entire

7

Maria Malibran, who, at the age of 17, created a sensation as Angelina in the first American performances, while her father's company visited New York. In a drawing by Hayter, 1829 (Opera Rara Collection)

Giuseppe de Begnis (in 1822), the creator of the role of Dandini (Opera Rara Collection)

work had to be staged. With Rossini producing masterpieces such as *Il barbiere*, *Otello*, and *La Cenerentola* under these conditions, it is less astonishing that he occasionally borrowed music from earlier operas than that he did not have recourse to this expedient more frequently.

Ever since *La cambiale di matrimonio* by the eighteen-year-old novice had its première at the Teatro San Mosé of Venice in 1810, Rossini was both master and victim of these extraordinary artistic conditions. Commissions poured in from theatres throughout northern Italy: *La pietra del paragone* and *Il Turco in Italia* for

Milan, *Tancredi* and *L'Italiana in Algeri* for Venice, and other works for Bologna and Ferrara. But in 1815 an event profoundly altered Rossini's career: Domenico Barbaja, impresario of the Teatro San Carlo in Naples, invited Rossini to establish residence there and to become musical director of the Neapolitan theatres. This proposal offered Rossini a permanent post and an escape from the excesses of his early career. Barbaja was crafty enough to allow Rossini freedom to compose for other cities, a temptation that at first proved appealing. From 1815 through 1817 he lived much as before, travelling from Naples to Rome and Milan, but from 1818 through 1822 Naples became his artistic home. Rossini could control his own schedule, allowing sufficient time for careful composition and production. His sojourn in Naples and the nature of the artists available there, however, were at least partly responsible for Rossini's abandoning altogether *opera buffa* to concentrate his efforts in the field of *opera seria*.

The composition of *La Cenerentola*, then, came at a crossroads in Rossini's career. He had begun to establish roots in Naples, but was still accepting commissions from other cities. His contract with the Teatro Valle for the Carnival season of 1817 had been signed the year before, on February 29, 1816, after the Roman première of *Il barbiere di Siviglia*. Rossini was supposed to write the opening opera of the season (December 26, 1816), and the theatre agreed to provide him with a libretto by October. Under the best of circumstances, then, Rossini would have been allowed little time, but in fact matters were much worse. Rossini's *Otello* did not have its Neapolitan première until December 4, 1816, so that the composer did not reach Rome until mid-December. The impresario, Pietro Cartoni, had presumably agreed that Rossini would write the second opera of the season instead of the opening one. We learn from the memoirs of Ferretti that the chosen libretto was entitled *Ninetta alla corte*, and was prepared by (Gaetano?) Rossi. Ferretti adds that the subject was actually *Francesca di Foix*, 'one of the least moral comedies of the French theatre in an epoch in which it was beginning to be known as an infamous school of libertinism . . . '* The ecclesiastical censors consequently insisted on so many changes that the libretto became incoherent, and Rossini, two days before Christmas, decided a new subject had to be found.

* Ferretti's report seems strange here and not completely reliable. *Ninetta alla corte* was presumably based on the libretto by Charles-Simon Favart, *Ninette à la cour*, first set to music in 1755, but better known at that time in the version adapted by August Creuzé de Lesser for Henri-François Berton. Berton's opera was first performed in Paris at the Opéra-Comique on December 21, 1811. *Francesca di Foix* is quite a different subject, based on a libretto by Jean-Nicolas Bouilly and Louis-Emmanuel Mercier-Dupaty, *Françoise de Foix*, set to music by Henri-Mouton Berton, father of Henri-François, and first performed at the Opéra-Comique on January 28, 1809. While both stories emphasize the dangers of court life for innocent young ladies, they are quite independent and it is difficult to imagine how they could have been combined into a single drama. *Françoise de Foix* ultimately did become an Italian opera, *Francesca di Foix* by Gaetano Donizetti, with a libretto by Domenico Gilardoni (Naples, Teatro San Carlo, May 30, 1831).

Gioachino Rossini

Pauline Viardot-Garcia, Maria Malibran's sister, who was a celebrated interpreter of La Cenerentola, singing it all over Europe and in St. Petersburg between 1830 and 1850 (Opera Rara Collection)

Ferretti was asked to provide the new libretto, and he and Rossini chose the subject of *Cinderella*. 'On Christmas day Rossini had the Introduzione. The cavatina of Don Magnifico on Saint Stephen's day (December 26); the duet for the tenor and soprano on San Giovanni (December 27). In short: I wrote the verses in *22* days and Rossini the music in *24*.' Rossini did have some assistance. Two arias (Alidoro's and Clorinda's) and a short chorus which opened Act II were the work of Luca Agolini, a Roman musician known mostly for his church music.* The secco recitative was also the work of another musician. But there is very little borrowed music in *La Cenerentola*: only the concluding section of the heroine's final rondò, '*Non più mesta accanto al fuoco*,' derived from the tenor aria in *Il barbiere di Siviglia*, '*Cessa di più resistere*,' and the Sinfonia, taken without change from *La gazzetta*. Rossini composed the remainder of this remarkable score in three weeks.

While Rossini's muse needed little external prodding in this collaboration, Ferretti's was another matter. In the author's preface to the original printing of his libretto, Ferretti excuses the quality of his verses, explaining that he had been compelled to write the text in a very short time. He then adds some words of explanation about the particular content of his version of the *Cinderella* story:

If Cinderella does not appear in the company of a wizard who works fantastic miracles or a talking cat, and does not lose a slipper at the ball (but instead gives away a bracelet), as in the French theatre or in some vast Italian theatre, it should not be considered a *crimenalesae* (an act of lese majesty) but rather a necessity of staging at the Teatro Valle and a gesture of respect for the delicacy of Roman taste which does not permit on the stage what might please in a fairy-tale beside the fire.

Ferretti omits, except by implication, a fundamental fact. His text is in large part derived from the libretto by Charles-Guillaume Etienne for Nicolò Isouard's *Cendrillon* (Paris, Opéra-Comique, February 22, 1810), as further filtered through the libretto that Felice Romani prepared for Stefano Pavesi's opera *Agatina o La virtù premiata*, which had its première in Milan at the Teatro alla Scala ('some vast Italian theatre') in April 1814.

Cendrillon is an *opéra comique*, the musical numbers separated not by recitative but by spoken dialogue. Etienne's libretto already has most of the characteristic elements of Ferretti's: the step-father and two step-sisters; the Prince's trusted councilor, Alidor; the masquerade in which the Prince exchanges positions with his servant, Dandini. Emphases are different, to be sure. The Baron of Montefiascone is not Rossini's buffoon, for such characters are foreign to the French tradition. The roles of the two sisters are

---

* For a revival of the opera at the Teatro Apollo of Rome during the Carnival season of 1821, Rossini himself composed a new aria for Alidoro, frequently performed today in place of Agolini's.

Luigi Lablache, a famous Dandini (Opera Rara Collection).

more fully developed by Etienne. But already in Isouard's opera the role of the supernatural is minimal. An enchanted sleep is used to plant the elegantly clothed Cendrillon at the ball. Otherwise the story is essentially as in Rossini and Ferretti. Cendrillon does lose a slipper (following Perrault) instead of handing over a bracelet, but Ferretti's substitution is surely due to the offended modesty of the Roman censors. There are many precise parallels. The opening scenes of the operas are, for example, essentially identical, with the two sisters admiring themselves, Cinderella singing a little ballad (*'Il était un p'tit homme'* or *'Una volta c'era un re'*), Alidoro asking for charity, which only Cinderella will give, etc.. Romani's libretto for Pavesi draws directly on Etienne, and Ferretti uses them both. Thus, to speak of Ferretti's having eliminated the magical effects of the *Cinderella* story makes no sense, for he worked not with Perrault's tale but with earlier operatic adaptations. Since the magical effects were absent from his sources, they were absent too in Ferretti.

The nature of its libretto makes this *Cenerentola* of Ferretti and Rossini significantly different from the comic operas Rossini had prepared before. The madcap hilarity of *L'Italiana in Algeri* and the wily, even raucous ways of Rosina in *Il barbiere di Siviglia* are no longer present in *La Cenerentola*. Don Magnifico and Dandini are, of course, comic characters in the great Italian tradition, with their solo buffo arias and their superb Act Two duet, *'Un segreto d'importanza,'* one of the finest buffo numbers in the entire repertory. But the principal characters, Cinderella herself and Don Ramiro, are sentimental, not comic characters. They are heirs of Richardson's *Pamela*, the virtuous servant girl loved and finally married by a noble patron (*Virtue rewarded* is Richardson's alternate title, *Goodness triumphant* is Ferretti's). And the earliest significant appearance of the sentimental genre in Italian opera is Nicolò Piccini's setting of Goldoni's *Pamela* imitation, *La buona figliola* (1760). From there through the remainder of the century *opera buffa* more and more frequently became the home for sentimental and pathetic heroines, expressing their sorrows and pleasures in a musically more simple and popular style.

This style characterizes much of Cenerentola's music, from her opening canzona, *'Una volta c'era un re,'* to her delightfully tentative and naive duet with Don Ramiro, *'Un soave non so che.'* Even when surrounded by the pure buffo declamation of others, as at the close of the *Introduzione*, Cenerentola emerges singing a beautifully soaring vocal line, *'Questo è proprio uno strapazzo!,'* which casts a radiance over the entire ensemble. But Rossini goes beyond even this style, until his heroine is hardly distinguishable from the protagonist of *Elisabetta, regina d'Inghilterra* (listen particularly to Cinderella's beautiful solo within the Act Two Quintet, *'Ah signor, s'è ver che in petto,'* and the *primo tempo* of her concluding *rondò*, *'Nacqui all'affanno e al pianto'*). *Opera buffa* here adapts for its own purposes not only the popular world of the sentimental *semiseria* genre but even the exalted vocal style of *opera seria* itself.

La Cenerentola, then, is far from the simple world of comic opera. In his next work, *La gazza ladra*, Rossini would carry *opera semiseria* beyond the comic sphere altogether. This change in genre, though partly related to the composer's Neapolitan experiences, was inherent in Italian opera of the period. Even in extra-Neapolitan commissions, Rossini did not choose comic plots; only in Paris would he again do so, but *Le Comte Ory* is far from the style of Italian *opera buffa*. Of all Rossini's operas, *La Cenerentola* is the most 'mixed' in genre, the broadest range of musical sources contributing to its rich style: the wealth and greatness of the opera is a direct function of that very diversity.

Because of the rapid preparation of *La Cenerentola*, there was little time for rehearsal, and the first performances were not well received. But, according to Ferretti, Rossini was undisturbed. The day after the fiasco, he told his depressed librettist:

> Fool! Before Carnival is done, everyone will be in love with it, before a year is up it will be sung from Lilibeo to Dora, and in two years it will please in France and astound the English. Impresarios will fight over it and, even more, so will prima donnas.

La Cenerentola did indeed have remarkable success during the nineteenth century. Although performed infrequently in the first decades of this century it never completely disappeared. In the Rossini revival since the war it has triumphantly reestablished itself as a repertory opera: a fairy story come true.

Concerning Christian-names

Dr Gossett has drawn attention to the common mis-spelling of Rossini's Christian name with two 'c's instead of the one 'c' (Gioachino) that he himself always used, and to the alternative Christian names of Giacomo and Jacopo attributed to the librettist, Ferretti, who used both on occasion. - Ed.

'La Cenerentola' (Cinderella)
A musical commentary

Arthur Jacobs

To tell the story clearly, to bring out the characters by musical means, and to please the listener by a succession of immediately attractive solos and ensembles — this combination was the required operatic formula of Rossini's time, and nowhere is it more brilliantly accomplished than in *La Cenerentola*. Not only brilliantly but subtly too. Here is not the pure comedy of *Il Barbiere di Siviglia*, founded on a traditional range of characters: in *La Cenerentola* pathos has its part as well.

Indeed the transformation of Cinderella from cruelly-used servant to triumphant princess is musically shown — she begins with a pathetic little ditty, sung to herself, and moves towards the brilliant 'public' coloratura of the aria with chorus which concludes the work. The heroine's real name in the opera, by the way, is Angelina. 'La Cenerentola', her nickname, derives from *cenere* (ashes), in the same way as Cinderella does from *cinders*; and the same is true of the French form *Cendrillon*, in the story by Perrault from which they both spring. The opening ditty is called a *canzone*, meaning in operatic terms a song that is 'really' sung by one of the characters (that is, it would be a song in real life or in a spoken play).

Cinderella's cruel stepsisters, though vain and silly, are different from the 'ugly sisters' of English pantomime. Other differences will be noted, particularly the absence of magic and the replacement of the fairy godmother by a prudent elderly adviser of the Prince's. The bibulous disposition of Cinderella's stepfather is hinted at in the title of his barony — 'Montefiascone' (Mountflagon). The use of only a *male* chorus was an economy which Italian theatres of the time appreciated.

Before the curtain rises Rossini provides his usual type of overture, a slow section followed by a faster [1, 2, 3] rising to a final climax: for the musical material of the climax, in this case, he borrows from the ensemble which ends the first act of the opera itself. Following the form favoured by Italian composers of that time for comic opera, the opera is in two acts — the first leading at curtain-fall to a situation of maximum complexity, musically involving all the main characters, and the second providing literally the *dénouement*, an 'un-knotting' of the tangle.

The libretto is a brilliant piece of work, and a tribute to its author, Jacopo Ferretti, is due from the present as translator of the English text used by the English National Opera. Such a libretto is written *for* music — not merely for setting line-by-line, but to fit

17

the successive types of musical form which the composer will wish to use. Ferretti accomplishes this neatly *and* writes clear, singable text free from inversions and stiffness — except where Dandini in disguise as the prince deliberately and comically pays court to Cinderella's step-sisters in absurdly high-flown style, comparing himself to the bee seeking the 'one sweetest flower' and then imploring them to release him, 'disarmed by Cupid's dart'.

The translator finds himself, indeed, constantly stimulated by the witty asides and ironies of the text. The only divergence in style which is to be found in the English version is this: Rossini ruthlessly repeats the Italian lines (for musical reasons), but where repetition blunts a comic point I have permitted myself to write new lines to sustain the fun — I hope.

The headings (e.g. 'Introduction', 'Aria') are those of the score, at this period always divided into separate numbers. Characters are named in order of singing within that number.

Act One
Scene One: The Baron's Mansion

Introduction. CLORINDA, TISBE, CINDERELLA, ALIDORO, CAVALIERS

No 'opening chorus', so often favoured in comic opera, is possible within the Baron's impoverished establishment. Cinderella's vain stepsisters are seen trying on some headgear and practising a dance-step [4]. They reprimand Cinderella for singing to herself her favourite song [5] about a king who chooses a true-hearted bride rather than a rich or beautiful one. A beggar (Alidoro, the prince's tutor, in disguise) enters, begging for alms. Spurned by the others, he is pitied by Cinderella, who gives him refreshment.

Now the chorus enters — cavaliers attached to the court of Prince Ramiro, who is staying at a palace nearby. They announce that the prince himself is to arrive to issue invitations to his grand ball[6]. Expressing their separate thoughts the four characters sing *with* the chorus to convey musically the sense of excitement and anticipation.

Recitative and cavatina: Don Magnifico. CLORINDA, CINDERELLA, ALIDORO, TISBE, DON MAGNIFICO

The invitation sets the stepsisters in a whirl[7]. They dismiss the 'beggar' rudely: before leaving he gives Cinderella a mysterious assurance that hers may yet be a happy fate. Cinderella goes to prepare her stepsisters' finery for the ball. The stepsisters quarrel as to which of them should have the right to tell the news to their father, the baron — when, unbidden and annoyed, he enters.

The following *cavatina* (in this sense an entrance aria) in one section without change of tempo, is the first big solo number of the opera. Don Magnifico, Baron Montefiascone, is a run-down aristocrat whose manners match those of his daughters, Clorinda and

18

Tisbe. Awakened from sleep by their chatter, he now narrates the dream he had, and his interpretation. The music begins with heavy repetitious phrases (*'Miei rampolli feminini'* — 'Why the devil did I get you as my offspring?') which mirror his annoyance and general boorishness; but by the end of the aria his prognostications of a change of fortune move him to fast, exhilarating music. In his dream he became an ass with feathers, flying to the top of a belfry — which he interprets as high promotion with each of the daughters marrying a prince. Excitedly, he imagines their royal babies prancing for the delight of their grandpa.

Recitative. CLORINDA, TISBE, DON MAGNIFICO

Informed of the prince's coming, Don Magnifico sees it as verification of his dream and primes his daughters for their royal encounter.

Scena and Duet: Cinderella and Don Ramiro. RAMIRO, CINDERELLA; OFF STAGE: CLORINDA, TISBE

Composers used the expression 'scena and . . . ' to cover the introductory conversational recitative to a formal solo, duet, etc.. Here Don Ramiro, Prince of Salerno (to give him his full title) enters in disguise as one of his own courtiers. Ordered by his father to marry, he has come to spy out the territory where he is to find his ideal bride in a daughter of the house — or so he has been assured by Alidoro, his tutor. Entering alone he first soliloquizes — speaking, in effect, to the audience. When at length Cinderella enters, bringing a cup of coffee for the baron, he takes her for a maid. Startled, she drops the cup.

The two are enchanted with each other [8a]. Finding it impossible to say so openly, they employ the operatic convention of the 'aside' (addressing the audience) — singing first in turn, then in harmony [8b]. The slow tempo breaks into fast as Ramiro finally asks the 'maid' where the Baron's daughters are, and receives a confused reply. The stepsisters' voices are heard. Cinderella must go to attend them, so she and the prince reluctantly bid each other farewell. (The change from slow to fast tempo, with a psychological change between — in this case, breaking from the 'asides' of love to routine conversation — forms one of the chief means by which such an opera as this progresses naturally within a scene.)

Recitative. RAMIRO, DON MAGNIFICO

Cinderella leaves. The baron enters briefly in haste and confusion. Ramiro now awaits the fulfilment of the 'other half' of the disguising: his confidential servant Dandini is to arrive and to pretend to be the prince.

Pages from Rossini's meticulously written manuscript score (Accademia Filarmonica, Bologna)

The sextet — Act One

The sextet — Act Two

Chorus and Cavatina: Dandini. COURTIERS, DANDINI, CLORINDA,
TISBE, DON MAGNIFICO, RAMIRO

Preceded by the courtiers, Dandini enters in princely dress and
hugely enjoys his pose. He sings in stately florid style [9] of his
royal quest for perfect beauty and then — as the stepsisters present
themselves, dressed up to kill — makes each of them believe he
adores her, with comic 'asides' to Ramiro.

Here occurs one of those masterly key-changes which Rossini
applies perfectly to the dramatic situation. Ignoring Ramiro's whis-
pered caution not to carry the deception too far, Dandini moves
with mock-sentimental passion from F to A flat to launch an appeal
to the girls: (*'Per pietà, quelle ciglia abbassate'* — 'Ah, have pity, oh,
spare those fatal glances . . . ').

All this is in the same rather slow tempo. Then a faster tempo
and a new tune take over as Dandini grows still more confident
(*'Ma al finir della nostra commedia'* — 'Oh, how easy I find them to
flatter') and the girls likewise feel sure of their conquest. All join
expressing their feelings. But it is still Dandini's number and he
remains the centre of attraction.

Recitative and Quintet. DANDINI, CLORINDA, DON MAGNIFICO,
RAMIRO, TISBE, CINDERELLA, ALIDORO.

One way in which the composer can make a scene progress has
already been indicated in this commentary: within an aria, a change
in mood or dramatic situation (even if it occurs only in the mind of
the character) can prompt a change of tempo from slow to fast, and
so increase the excitement. In this number the same procedure is
used but on a larger scale. A recitative involving six characters
leads (with the disappearance of two) to a formal quartet, in which
Cinderella pleads with Don Magnifico to let her as well as her stepsisters go to the ball (Dandini and Ramiro overhearing and com-
menting). Then Alidoro in a new guise enters, changing the
dramatic situation and prompting a new strain of music (a quintet)
— itself having a slow, then a fast section. The whole number has,
moreover, a unified key-structure just as would be found in an instrumental movement of comparable length.

We may now describe this number in more detail. In an introductory recitative, Dandini in disguise as the prince narrates (in
comic multiple rhyme) his father's command that he should marry.
To that end he has invited all the unmarried ladies of the district to
a ball. Clorinda and Tisbe, escorted by the cavaliers, leave for the
palace. But as Don Magnifico prepares to go with him, Cinderella
detains him imploringly — will he not take her as well, even for an
hour, half an hour, a quarter of an hour [10]? He pushes her away
and threatens her with his cane, to the disgust of Ramiro and
Dandini — these four voices being displayed in a formal quartet.
Cinderella's vocal line is both pleading and (as she thinks of the

dazzle of the ball) florid and excited: even within the demands of the ensemble, Rossini provides a touching musical portrayal of her character.

The quartet ends with apparent finality. Cinderella is *not* to be taken to the ball. With three heavy unison strokes of the keynote C the orchestra confirms it — when suddenly an unprepared change of key (chord of E flat) marks the unexpected appearance of Alidoro. He comes as an official bearing a register, from which it appears that *three* sisters, and not two, inhabit this dwelling. His measured questioning demands a slower pace. The third sister 'died', says Don Magnifico, while Cinderella can scarcely stammer a protest.

A further change of key (to A flat) brings the formal quintet in which Don Magnifico, Cinderella and Dandini in turn remark in slow time on how the face of each one present reveals the doubts within [11]. Then a more active mood seizes them (Don Magnifico sarcastically bullying Cinderella) — a mood expressed with a change of rhythm, a suddenly faster tempo, *and* a return to the opening key (C major). The spectator is perhaps conscious only of the developing story and the succession of agreeable, contrasting musical strains — but this 'works' only because Rossini's mastery as composer has found the technical means to articulate a long musical structure which covers all the expression needed by all the characters. Finally Don Magnifico leaves for the royal palace, as do Dandini and Ramiro.

Recitative. ALIDORO, CINDERELLA.

Left behind with Cinderella, Alidoro gently surprises her. He will bring her to the ball and supply her costume and jewels. 'What's this, a play?' she asks, bewildered. Alidoro's reply is one that the translator cannot resist adapting into: 'Yes, my daughter, all the world's a stage, and all the men and women merely players'.*

Scene Two: The Prince's Palace

First Finale. COURTIERS, DON MAGNIFICO, RAMIRO, DANDINI, CLORINDA, TISBE, ALIDORO, CINDERELLA.

The 'first finale' (i.e. finale to Act One) is, in this type of comic opera, the longest and most complex single item of the score, presenting all the main characters in various vocal combinations. Don Magnifico has amazed the courtiers (or they pretend to amazement) by his drinking capacity, in token of which he is apparently

---

* For a performance in 1821, Rossini wrote a fine aria for Alidoro. This is some-times performed, so the alternative words have been included in the libretto (page 66), and Colin Graham's comments upon them may be read on page 38. Agolini composed an aria to follow the recitative for the first performance. Entitled '*Vasto teatro è il mondo*', it is still included in the Ricordi vocal score. (Ed.)

to be made the prince's steward. He dictates — while the courtiers write it down — an absurd proclamation against mixing wine with water. Rossini uses here with particular aptness the device of giving a catchy tune not to the singer but to the orchestra, while the 'dictation' goes for long periods on a monotone [17].*

In another room, Prince Ramiro and Dandini meet in haste. Dandini, still dressed as the prince, and pursued by the stepsisters, snatches a word with Ramiro to warn him of how odious the girls are. The musical point of this comic duet is not only its 'scampering' but its confidential whispering, with many repetitions of '*zitto*' ('quiet!'), '*piano*' ('softly!') and '*sotto voce*'. The scampering pace is maintained not only by the voices but by the orchestral violins [13].

The same scampering music continues when the stepsisters 'catch' Dandini. He protests that he cannot marry two, so he will choose one and bestow the other on . . . his squire (pointing to the real prince). The stepsisters reject such a 'low-class' alliance with scorn, even when Ramiro now begs them to marry him. This is the supremely ironic moment of the plot — and one which is recalled towards the end of the opera.

The ball proper is about to begin when the mood (and the key) changes. An off-stage chorus (from the entrance hall of the palace) announces the arrival of a beauty. Alidoro's announcement that she is veiled deepens the suspense. The stepsisters, suspecting a beautiful rival for the prince's affections, are alarmed. It is, of course, Cinderella — dazzling in appearance and unrecognized. Matching this dazzle she introduces herself with a florid declamation '*Sprezzo quei don che versa fortuna capricciosa*', literally 'I set no value on those gifts which fickle fortune bestows', operatically translated 'All is not gold that glitters'[14].

Then she unveils. Moment of astonishment (and change of key! — E flat to G). In the succeeding ensemble Rossini re-employs, as in the earlier quintet, the device of successive characters entering with the same expression of perplexity: '*Parlar, pensar vorrei . . .*' — 'I'd like to speak my feelings, but words will not be found' [15]. Don Magnifico, till now absent (in the wine-cellar!) enters and joins the astonishment. *Can* it be Cinderella? Dandini rallies his guests — time to go within for supper and dancing.

But before they do so, a mood of wonder again strikes the company. In a hushed unison, each speaking for himself or herself, they compare their situation to being in an idyllic garden suddenly hit by a tempest [16]. This 'poetic' fancy has a strictly musical point — after a quiet beginning, the gathering 'tempest' is represented in a *crescendo* over an insistent rhythm. The music sinks

* Don Magnifico's recitative and aria [17] are sometimes (as at ENO) used to open the second act, instead of a chorus '*Ah della bella incognita*' of which only a manuscript survives, written by Agolini for the first performance, and which is not generally performed at all, or Rossini's own aria written for Magnifico at that point. (Ed.)

down but revives, repeated and extended, as an exhilarating end to the act.

Act Two

Scene One: The Prince's Palace

Recitative and aria*: Don Magnifico. DON MAGNIFICO, TISBE, CLORINDA.

The baron and his daughters review the situation. Upset as they are by the appearance of the unknown beauty, they are still confident of capturing the prince. Whichever of the two wins him, the baron will be sure of a powerful position as go-between at court, with handsome bribes (in money or food) from those anxious to procure a royal favour. He imagines an interview between himself and a female petitioner (imitating her in falsetto) and then, in rapid patter, sees himself as so surrounded by other petitioners that he has to shut the door on them.

Recitative, scena and aria: Don Ramiro. TISBE, CLORINDA, RAMIRO, DANDINI, CINDERELLA, ALIDORO, COURTIERS.

Dandini, still acting as Prince Ramiro, has himself been smitten by Cinderella's charms. But she turns his compliments aside, confessing that she is in love with his 'squire' (that is, the real prince). But when Ramiro appears she turns aside his declaration too: she gives him a bracelet and says that when he finds its companion-piece, *then* she will be his. She leaves. Alidoro encourages the prince to pursue the prompting of his heart. Suddenly resolute, Ramiro tells Dandini the charade of impersonation is over: he orders his coach and prepares to set out and find her.

An aria in three sections, with chorus of his courtiers, expresses his new mood: first expressing determination, in almost martial music [18a], then passing to a gentler strain as he contemplates the bracelet and thinks of its owner, then again resolute [18b]. (The tenor's top C is strongly used in both first and third sections.) Ramiro and his courtiers depart.

Recitative and duet: Dandini and Don Magnifico. ALIDORO, DANDINI, DON MAGNIFICO.

Alidoro, intending to promote his plan by making the prince's coach break down near the baron's house, hastens off. Dandini remains behind, peevishly fretting that he is now an 'ex-prince'. The baron enters, pressing the 'prince' (as he still assumes Dandini to be) for a decision on whether Clorinda or Tisbe is to be the lucky bride. Dandini, affecting an air of tremendous secrecy, promises to tell him what has happened [19]. (The Italian librettist, with the English translator following, uses what must be an old joke. DON

---

* This piece is not always performed. Don Magnifico's 'dictation' aria is used to open the second act instead. It is not included in the libretto. (Ed.)

MAGNIFICO: 'I stand on tip-toe!' DANDINI: 'Then take a seat, I beg you'.)

The air of comic confidences is repeated musically in duet, with short, detached vocal ejaculations. Dandini asks him what comforts his daughter would expect — the baron demands the highest honours — and Dandini explains that far from this, as his wife she would live only on the sevants' level, for he himself is only a valet and what has passed was only a masquerade. As the baron's incredulity gives way to outrage, the music changes from a moderately quick 4/4 to a quicker 6/8. The baron's indignation is in vain and Dandini teases him: 'I'll have my rights!' — 'Right through the door!'

Recitative: ALIDORO.

It is a stormy night — which will aid the plan for the breakdown of the carriage, and the eagerness of the prince for departure was another happy portent. (This recitative is a useful 'cover' for a scene-change rather than dramatically vital.)

Scene Two: The Baron's Residence

Song: Cinderella

The Italian word 'canzone' (see above, p.17) is now used by the composer to denote Cinderella's little ditty, previously heard within the opening number [5]. Its repetition here is a simple, touching way of indicating that superficially Cinderella's situation is as before — her clothes, the setting, and her apparent mood are again those of the downtrodden servant, as at the opening of the opera.

Recitative and Storm. CINDERELLA, CLORINDA, DON MAGNIFICO, TISBE.

But all is *not* the same. She looks lovingly at the bracelet and thinks of the attractive suitor (the prince's squire, as she still supposes) who possesses its companion. Her stepsisters and the baron enter crossly. She pretends not to know why, and goes at their bidding to prepare a meal. Outside a storm is brewing and the orchestra depicts it — fast, loud, agitated music rising to a climax, then subsiding to gentleness (and the minor turning into a 'smiling' major key) as the elements become peaceful again.

Recitative and Sextet. DANDINI, DON MAGNIFICO, DON RAMIRO, CLORINDA, CINDERELLA, TISBE.

The royal carriage has broken down. Dandini, as part of the prince's escort, stumbles into this as the nearest house — not realizing for a moment, that it is the baron's. Despite the embarrassment of this further meeting with Dandini, the Baron is sure it betokens an interest in his daughters' prospects. Astonished to learn that the 'attendant' Ramiro is the true prince, Don Magnifico and the girls are even more astonished when — noticing the

25

matched bracelets — the prince claims Cinderella.

The sextet begins with the same phrase from Dandini, Ramiro, Don Magnifico and Cinderella in succession. Detached notes seem to represent the distracted, surprised thoughts of each [20]. On top of this Clorinda and Tisbe, who have been silent, suddenly make *their* puzzlement heard. The slow, measured pace (the indication is *maestoso*, 'majestically') allows the unrolling of florid coloratura by one character at a time, paralleling the verbal emphasis on the feeling that one's head is spinning.

Abruptly, the suspense is broken (and the tempo is changed to a faster one) as Clorinda turns accusingly on Cinderella, followed by Don Magnifico. With superior weight Ramiro now turns on them. In slower tempo and with a shift of key, as though to establish a reconciliation, Cinderella asks Ramiro [21] to have mercy on her tormentors — but they call her a hypocrite and Don Magnifico tries to re-establish the claims of his daughters. Ramiro sarcastically quotes back at them (in music and words!) the disparagement they flung at him in Act One when he offered himself to them. He formally invites Cinderella to be his consort; she tries once again to gain her stepfather's and stepsisters' good-will and is once again repulsed. The sustained tension is manifested in an insistent strain [22] for all six characters, itself in that 'doubled dynamic' form (soft to loud, sinking down, then rising again to an even greater climax) which forms a cherished constructive device of Rossini's.

Recitative. TISBE, CLORINDA, ALIDORO

The stepsisters realize the game is up. Alidoro enters and reveals that he was the 'beggar' whom they repulsed and Cinderella pitied. (In the Italian he now refers to her by her real name, Angelina.) The baron's property will have to be sold, as he has squandered Cinderella's dowry. He and his daughters will be impoverished unless they beg Cinderella's pardon. Clorinda flounces off, but Tisbe resolves to apologize: 'I prefer humble pie to plain starvation'. Alidoro, who has already made all the arrangements for an immediate wedding, is well content.

Scene Three: A Room with a Throne

Chorus, Scena and Rondò-Finale: Cinderella. COURTIERS, RAMIRO, CINDERELLA, DON MAGNIFICO, DANDINI, CLORINDA, TISBE [AND ALIDORO].

Fortune's wheel has turned, as the chorus of courtiers proclaim, assembling to welcome their new princess. All are to witness 'the triumph of goodness' — which, as 'il trionfo della bontà,' is the subtitle of the opera. Cinderella, led in by Don Ramiro, is 'stupefied by joy' (in the words of the stage direction). The baron and his daughters have by this time *all* realized the prudence of apology. Cinderella asks her consort to allow her the royal privilege of 'revenge' (with a big, 'menacing' flourish in the vocal line) — but her 'revenge' is 'to grant them pardon'.

The final item of the opera now follows. It is a long, brilliant aria with chorus — that is, with the unified support of all the other characters as well as the chorus proper. (By an apparent oversight, no part for Alidoro is given in the score, but he would naturally join in the line of his fellow-bass, Don Magnifico.)

For reasons that are obscure, the term *rondò* (we reproduce the correct Italian spelling, with accent on the second syllable) is applied by composers of Italian opera at this and an earlier period to a certain type of compound aria-form without reference to the usual significance of the term in instrumental music. Instrumentally, the form implies the recurrence of one main strain with diverse episodes between. Operatically, as in Fiordiligi's *'Per pietà'* from Mozart's *Così fan tutte*, no such recurrence is found: instead, a spacious slow section is followed by an equally imposing fast section. So here Cinderella begins with a slow 6/8, *'Nacqui all'affanno e al pianto'*, 'Born to a life that was lonely' [23a] — where, with a coloratura flourish, she compares her transformation to a stroke of lightning [23b]. Then, *allegro*, she asks the baron and his daughters not to cry ('No, no, no, no'). She wants only to embrace, to forgive, to be reconciled. The reaction of the courtiers to her kindness prepares for her second strain within the *allegro* tempo. This is the principal part of the aria, beginning *'Non più mesta accanto al fuoco'*, 'Now no longer by the cinders' [23c]. Starting as a simple catchy tune, it proceeds to elaborate vocal variations with choral accompaniment.

The demands on the mezzo-soprano voice include the just-over-two-octave run from high A to low G sharp, and (as a climax) a top B above this. Such brilliant display makes its own appeal but Rossini's feat is — here as in the rest of the opera — to have placed and timed his music perfectly for the realization of story and character.

Della Jones as Cinderella at English National Opera (photo: Reg Wilson)

'Cinderella' in perfomance

There is much debate as to how Rossini's operas should be performed. I took the opportunity of the ENO production of 'Cinderella' to talk to the conductor and producer about performing 'Cinderella' in English for today's audience, and about the musical and theatrical conventions on which Rossini relied, as well as those which have since developed. — Ed.

I — A Conversation with Mark Elder

Mark Elder, ENO Music Director, went to his first opera when he was ten years old (and still a choirboy at Canterbury Cathedral) at Glyndebourne where he subsequently began his professional career. Glyndebourne's remarkable standard of ensemble singing was cultivated by Vittorio Gui, Fritz Busch and Jani Strasser in the years after 1945 on the Mozart and Rossini repertory. Mark Elder has since treasured the Rossini masterpieces, and conducted 'The Italian Girl in Algiers', as well as 'Cinderella', at the London Coliseum.

N.J. What would you tell someone coming to *Cinderella* for the first time to look out for?

M.E. Well, for me, the overriding characteristic of a performance of any Rossini score, whether comic or serious, is that it must give the impression of being a spontaneous, improvised entertainment. Rossini's operas do not fall into any preconceived patterns; and this is particularly true of the comic ones. Their most arresting features, which may be called 'Rossinian', are not rooted in the past. They have certain predecessors in the complicated ensembles of Cimarosa and Mozart, yet in masterpieces such as *Cinderella* and *The Barber* Rossini produced a world of his own, an imaginative scheme that is quite without parallel. The performers have to create an atmosphere where anything might happen, and to communicate this fantasy world to the public. An audience can never be sure how Rossini will cope with a situation, but the performers should appear to have no problems, just as though they were artists in a vocal and dramatic circus.

N.J. — In the sense that the coloratura is 'acrobatic' singing?

M.E Yes. Singing is, after all, an athletic exercise. Rossini's music gives singers wonderful opportunities to display technique and to give the audience the impression that they are creating the music and experimenting all the time. I do not, however, believe that singers should add their own virtuoso displays. (It might be worth pointing out here that, apart from three bars added by Rossini to the finale for the sake of extra brilliance, no music has been added in our performance.) A feature of recent performances of *La Cenerentola* has been the existence of Alberto Zedda's edition of the

29

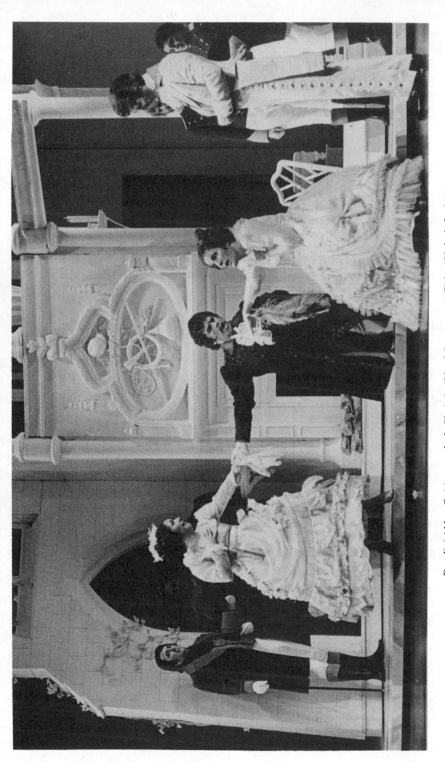

Dandini (Alan Opie) courts both Clorinda (Meryl Drower) and Tisbe (Shelagh Squires) simultaneously while their proud father (Richard Van Allan) looks on. (photo: Reg Wilson)

score, based on Rossini's manuscript, which is itself remarkable for its clarity. Zedda has, so to speak, used a strong detergent to clean it right out, removing a lot of the traditions which used to be accepted without question. Although I was surprised by some of Zedda's decisions, I can now see the reasons for them. There is, for example, no percussion part — one might argue because Rossini was writing for a theatre small enough not to need one. Yet there is a trombone in almost every number, giving a little more definition and spice to the bass part. The string section is that required for Mozart. Zedda's revisions make the texture more transparent, providing, for example, more interesting work for the two piccolos (not just one). He has swept away all later additions, including notes added to the harmonies and parts for instruments which Rossini did not use. This removes a layer of pastry, as it were, from the music which should be light and buoyant.

N.J. Do you think the very quiet opening of the overture, sometimes scarcely audible in a restless auditorium, is effective?

M.E. Rossini's contribution to the operatic overture stems from his desire to stimulate, entertain, surprise and, sometimes, to shock. His musical sense of humour is his most distinctive feature, and it is communicated with the most economic of means. The opening bar of this overture is extraordinarily unexpected: it sounds as though half the orchestra is missing. Then, with the full orchestra chords that follow we realise that the whole effect was intended to intrigue us. In the overture to *Il Signor Bruschino*, a little-known one-act opera, he calls for the violins to tap the music-stands with their bows, in order to attract attention. It created a minor sensation when first done, because the audience felt the composer was laughing at them. These are deliberate musical outrages, trademarks of Rossini's personality.

N.J. The evening is certainly full of musical jokes. One that springs to mind is the curious exclamation of dismay which Clorinda and Tisbe utter in the Act Two sextet: even if we cannot make out the words ('Hear them moan and hear them mutter'), we immediately appreciate their annoyance.

M.E. Rossini's musical imagination stops at nothing. One of the great challenges for performers is to give the impression that his music is the most natural and most suitable for that moment. His ensembles (sometimes for six, seven, eight or even nine singers) produce a wonderful effect, rather like a family team of acrobats contributing to a great tableau. One character may have a lyrical melody, four others may be chattering or whispering and two others may be making love on the quiet: the whole effect is vivacious and exhilarating. Just before the moment you mentioned (which is incidentally very difficult to sing cleanly), he transforms the scene into a bubble of time. Each character, one by one, repeats

31

'*Questo è un nodo avviluppato*' ('Here's a plot there's no denying'). Each syllable is pronounced separately and softly, and when performers create this *staccato* effect with the right tension, it seems as if time stands still.

N.J. Another such moment is Alidoro's entrance to announce Cinderella's arrival at the ball. The audience seem to grasp what is going on only after he has deflected three urgent questions, such as 'What's her name?'.

M.E. That is a good example of Rossini's treatment of an entirely prosaic text. He is so great an operatic composer because he has transformed words which were not remarkable on the page into an extended sequence of laughter. We sense in a successful performance that the lines seem to be delayed and that the audience cannot wait for the next question, on account of the orchestral 'giggles' between each question and answer.

N.J. Do you set about rehearsing a Rossini score in a different way from Verdi or Puccini?

M.E. Yes. The challenge is to obtain the right combination of fantasy and discipline. The ensembles are obviously very difficult to sing *exactly* together: the music is of sufficient simplicity that it is relatively easy to sing to a certain standard, but the challenge is to rise above that level with spirit and precision. Whether for only a few notes, or for several pages, these ensembles demand weeks of rehearsal. The singers have to work gradually towards a feeling of sharing it both in musical and human terms. They must be humble enough to work selflessly: the ultimate test of a great artist. This ensemble technique is valuable for Mozart and Donizetti also, and, of course, Mozart's scores explore a deeper range of human emotion altogether.

N.J. Are Rossini's operas difficult to cast?

M.E. It is hard to find a perfectly matched team to achieve this all-important unity. It would be no solution to employ two great principals of international class with a couple of days' rehearsal in addition to five company artists. Rossini singers must have, in addition to power and agility, a lightness and fantasy in their voices, so that the music does not sound like overcooked suet!

N.J. Rossini used to complain that singers were increasingly making their voices perform like instruments. It might seem to today's audiences that Rossini asks for singers just with virtuoso technique.

M.E. The challenge for singers is to develop the bravura technique and then to align it with an imaginative concept so that it seems that at any particular moment this is the most *natural* thing to be doing. For instance, when Cinderella and Ramiro meet for the first time, they both have a number of ecstatic embellishments, in-

32

tended to illustrate their delight and surprise. Mozart would have written this, perhaps, as a more sustained passage; Rossini makes it breathless and gentle. It can easily sound too instrumental. It is, of course, interesting that Rossini wanted to avoid this happening.

N.J. The Act One finale must also be an unusually difficult passage to make seem convincing on the stage.

M.E. It requires on the part of both audience and performers a degree of fantasy that knocks us sideways, because it is so unexpected. We laugh at the sheer pleasure of it: there seems at that point to be magic and tension in the air.

N.J. In performance it still works, even for today's audience unused to Rossini's conventions. Are you aware that it takes us a little time to 'get into' the spirit of the music?

M.E. The theatre's capacity to draw the audience in to share an experience is remarkable. (It always takes me twenty minutes, when I go to see a Western, to understand what anyone is saying!) This is why the role of the overture or prelude is so interesting: if it is well written, it can prepare us for the type of theatre we are about to experience. This introduction need not be only musical. For example, the East German producer, Joachim Herz, placed a broken-down car outside the Komische Oper in East Berlin before his new production of *Mahagonny*, which opens after a car has broken down in the desert. This intrigues an audience. Rossini's operas have a great place in our theatre because they also intrigue viewers to enter another world.

N.J. Would you like to comment on Rossini's characteristic habit of repeating phrases?

M.E. A characteristic of Italian is to repeat phrases not only for emphasis but to convey different shades of meaning. Look at the many examples of repeated phrases in the operas of Verdi or Puccini. Rossini did not repeat words, in my opinion, because there was a lack of text to set but because he wanted to make a specific point or comic effect.

N.J. What sort of orchestral playing do you find is necessary for Rossini?

M.E. It is a tightrope act. The orchestration is of a delicacy that demands a balance of poise and flexibility. For the string players, particularly the violins, it is an evening of *spiccato* — bouncing the bow on the string. The coordination of finger and bow demands great technique, particularly in fast music. It is just as hard as to sing it correctly, and few people understand this, including the players themselves! The woodwind has to combine lyrical beauty and supreme elegance with a sharp wit. So often is the wind called upon to comment on the stage action, that the wind players stand

'Alboni is not an 'artiste' to startle the multitude by dramatic intensity or the outbreak of passion. Her indolence of action, and apathy in the concerted pieces, afford little notion of the excitement of the passing scene, but when once a simple melody is to be breathed forth, with quiet pathos, the ecstasy at her lovely organ is unbounded, and Alboni's triumph is sure'. Or as 'The Times' observed (May 2, 1848) 'her figure is not exactly calculated to represent the gifted favourite of the good fairy'.

out like characters in the drama. This constant alternation between the two colours poses a great challenge to the players.

N.J. I noticed that you called a lot of recitative rehearsals.

M.E. In order to achieve the necessary flow in the recitatives, it is essential for the singers to repeat them often enough for them to become second nature. Performers must enjoy the business of delivering them, responding to each other by a subconscious reflex. Our recitative rehearsals are similar to the way actors may speak through a scene together in a canteen, without any energy or expression; or to the limbering-up of a ballet dancer.

N.J. Do you change the note-values in recitative to suit the words of the translation?

M.E. I believe there should be a clear demarcation between declamation and lyrical expression. (The composers of the late 19th century who merge them make this increasingly difficult but the classic art from Monteverdi onwards was based on this juxtaposition of fantasy and precision.) In recitative, by and large, the musical rhythms have no empiric value of their own and exist only as a natural frame-work to the text. The rhythm can be altered to suit the translation. By contrast, in the lyrical passages, nothing must hinder the original music. After all, the reason why the composer did not set the words originally to a melodic arch was because the line was to be recited or declaimed — as opposed to *arioso*, which is 'strung through the air' according to musical values. The combination of the *cantante* and recitative is the crux of the style.

N.J. Do you, yourself, feel exhilarated after a performance?

M.E. After a good performance certainly. The immediate feeling is elation, even inspiration, especially after the last scene of *La Cenerentola*. The tiredness comes some hours later.

N.J. Do you occasionally find yourself restraining the performers in performance — not just keeping them together, but actually maintaining a control with a return to quiet dynamics and a rock steady rhythm for ensembles? These could at first seem abnormally quiet and slow to an audience, which does not know what is to follow.

M.E. An example might be the famous sextet '*Parlar, pensar vorrei*' ('I'd like to speak my feelings'). We have to suggest curiosity and tension in the entries of Clorinda and Ramiro, so that Cinderella's brilliant notes flower naturally and spontaneously. The variation between loud and soft dynamics is also very marked in Rossini; the performance has to be carefully prepared so that in itself it is a liberation. But the audience must not feel that the conductor is holding back the performers. The relationship of rhythm and dynamics must be perfectly calculated so that the fast and loud sections fit into the general pattern. Sometimes, of course, per-

Elizabeth Inverarity, who sang Cinderella in 'The Fairy Queen or The Little Glass Slipper' at Covent Garden in 1831, at the age of seventeen. (Covent Garden Archives)

formers forget and I have to remind them of what we rehearsed. This discipline cannot be devised in performance; it must be firmly fixed, like the foundation of a house; you can't build on sand.

II — A Conversation with Colin Graham

Colin Graham is ENO Director of Productions, Director of Productions at the Opera Theatre of St Louis and founder-director of the English Music Theatre. He first produced 'Cinderella' in this translation for Scottish Opera in 1969, and then directed a new production for EMT, which toured Britain in 1976-8, before it was taken over by ENO for performances at the London Coliseum.

N.J. You once said to me that, in your opinion, *Cinderella* was the most human of Rossini's operas. Would you care to expand on that?

C.G. I am not a great lover of Rossini's operas, although I do love his music, because I find none of them, except Cinderella, particularly amusing; they are brittle and heartless, and about cardboard, artificial people. But *Cinderella* is a very human story, about a tender person with real problems, and the music, like some passages from *Count Ory*, has for me much greater depths than Rossini's other scores.

N.J. Cinderella is a really delightful character, and not just downtrodden.

C.G. She is not merely a household drudge but very much a member of the family and stands up for herself, as for instance, in the opening scene when she insists on singing her song. Also, we can tell from her observations at the ball that she is getting some fun out of the other characters' reactions to her appearance! The question of loving someone 'for himself alone' is also treated in a very sensitive and satisfactory way. And when the family returns to the Baron's mansion, she is delightfully ingenuous, asking 'What have I done?', now that her new-found love strengthens her ability to cope with them more effectively than before.

N.J. Are you attached to the piece essentially because of this central character?

C.G. I love and have always loved the story itself. It's one of those stories that is part of childhood and yet full of eternal truths. It's very important to be true to this aspect in all the characterisation. The sisters, for instance, must not be caricatures. If you strip away pantomime preconceptions about them, and just listen to the music, you find they both have great character. They argue about the one's superiority over the other: Clorinda is the elder, and sharper, while Tisbe is almost as put upon as Cinderella by her sister! They are both vain and silly, but they are believable people.

N.J. Like their father . . . ?

C.G. You could say that Rossini's musical conception of Don Magnifico makes him the most 'buffo' figure of all, but he is actually an extremely complicated character. At face value, he is very unpleasant. His entrance aria has to be examined carefully to discover why he is called Magnifico.

N.J. He has delusions of grandeur —

C.G. Yes, he has an overblown idea of himself, but at the same time he is able to say to his daughters that 'anyone can tell by looking at you two that your father must have been a donkey!' Such a perceptive remark is not at all 'buffo'. The absence of the cruel step-mother of traditional pantomime, where the father is a comically incapable old man, throws the burden here on the father to be the controlling element in the household: he has to be harsh yet, at the same time, absurd.

N.J. What about the other characters?

C.G. Another unusual feature for a comic Italian opera is Ramiro's relationship to his tutor, Alidoro. Ramiro is a boy who actually grows up in the course of the opera. Even Dandini has his profounder moments — when he falls in love with Cinderella at the ball and regrets that he is not a prince, and cannot have her. You might say that this is reminiscent of Beaumarchais. They *can* all be played *buffo*, of course; but the opera is not called *melodramma giocoso* for nothing: *opera buffa* would be quite a different matter.

N.J. Do you find Alidoro rather a disappointing character?

C.G. No. He must be cast from strength. His philosophy is remarkable, and he expands this particularly in the aria, when he comes to take Cinderella to the ball. He constantly refers to the powers which control everyone's destiny, and expands on this pantheistic version in part of the aria which we do not perform at ENO, because the role is taken by a baritone, whereas the omitted section demands a true *basso cantante*. The singer who took the role for ENO (Geoffrey Chard) at first thought of the character as a secondary part but came to appreciate its richness and depth, and the absolute necessity for it to be cast with a performer of stature and a creative acting talent.

N.J. Apart from cutting part of Alidoro's aria, in ENO performances Don Magnifico's drinking aria with chorus, '*Intendente, reggitor?*', is moved from the opening of the first act finale to the beginning of the second act.

C.G. This is a traditional arrangement in this country — Glyndebourne and the old Sadler's Wells production followed it. The first act already lasts for an hour and a half and this number would increase it to almost an hour and three-quarters. At the

Coliseum (though not with EMT) for reasons of length, we also omit the central section from the second act sextet, in which Cinderella pleads with Ramiro not to be too hard on Clorinda, Tisbe and Don Magnifico. This I very much regret because it lessens the effect of her forgiveness in the final scene, making this moment rather more superficial. We also ignore the aria written by Agolini for Clorinda — it is an *aria del sorbetto*, so-called because the audience could take the opportunity of some music of indifferent quality to eat an ice-cream, and it comes much too late in the opera.

N.J. Does the regular repetition of lines create problems for you?

C.G. Not for me really: the producer and singer have to find reasons for the repeats to elucidate the text. It posed a problem initially for the translator, who preferred in many cases to write new lines instead of repetitions, in the style of what he conceived would have been there if the music had been set to an English original. Mark Elder persuaded him to accept, somewhat reluctantly, a verbal repetition instead at some points. Although such a change removed much of the wit of the translation (we *used* that wit in the English Music Theatre production), I understood the conductor's reasoning. However, I don't think we have yet solved the problem: the *first* line of a rhyming couplet nearly always sets up the resolution of the second, which is the *close* of the rhyme. If you merely repeat the first line, you are invariably repeating an unsatisfactory line. Arthur Jacobs, who made this excellent translation many years ago now, might have preferred to have rewritten the lines in question to ensure an elegant and witty line which would be to the point and *bear* the repetition. But I understand that he maintains his original view, and his text has certainly engaged the responses of audiences at productions of the opera by different companies over the years.

N.J. Do you find this sort of artificial comedy has its problems for you?

C.G. As I have already said, although it is a naive story, the characters are not at all artificial. Yet it is not a comedy of manners, and it is difficult to hit the right degree of comedy in the acting. We have to appreciate the difference between real comedy and farce: *Cinderella*, unlike the 'buffo' *Italian Girl* or *Barber*, is not farce. The text has a very steely edge to it.

N.J. Rossini's habit of suspending the action for an ensemble is very striking. How do you ask the cast to play these passages?

C.G. Of course, this kind of moment happens often in opera. And during Shakespeare's soliloquies time stands still while the characters are immersed in reflection. This can be shown on stage (as it is in this production) by a sudden stillness, and a change of lighting. There is, nevertheless, a danger that long ensembles, such as Rossini's, can become dead if the characters are static. A *frisson* must stay in the air, the characters must remain aware of each other thoughout. They should not retreat too far into their 'Stanislavsky bubbles'.

N.J. Mark Elder also mentioned the importance of rehearsing the ensemble.

C.G. It is essential in this genre: there is no room for 'stars'. Every moment is important and each effect must be calculated to the last detail.

N.J. Would you say it is as demanding as, say, Mozart?

C.G. It is definitely more difficult to direct than Mozart, in order to achieve the correct level of comedy. As for the performers, the most severe test is the all-important appearance of spontaneity, which is the product of concentrated rehearsals with a committed ensemble.

N.J. What do you make of the storm?

C.G. Rossini seems to have had a predilection for storms. This one helps the plot along and it is very charming that, when Alidoro says that he has arranged everything, he implies the weather as well! And it is musically much more attractive than the storm in *The Barber* which is, if anything, even more gratuitous. It provides a much-needed orchestral interlude, following the chatter and plot in the act so far. (We play it as an exterior scene: it must seem odd played as an interior of the Baron's house.)

N.J. Would you like to say something about Roger Butlin's set?

C.G. It was conceived in this light way to match the, shall I say, pellucid character of the score. The white set and off-white costumes also balance and counteract the darkness of the plot: the music sparkles throughout, despite the harshness of some of the words. A grim stone kitchen would not be appropriate.

N.J. This set is particularly apt because it is intriguing. Audiences like to see it revolve, pushed by members of the cast.

C.G. That is part of the man-made magic of a show which has no pumpkin turning into a coach and dissolving ball-dress. We wanted a substitute for pantomime magic. The revolve also provides the six necessary scenes in quick succession without a curtain. It depends for its effect on lighting — another aspect of the man-made magic, if you like. For example, when the offstage chorus annouce Cinderella's arrival, all the lights dim to a romantic blue, full of anticipation and mystery. Then the courtiers enter in red velvet coats, and the candelabra are brought in. The contrasts of colour and light are magical in themselves.

40

N.J. This leads to the curious first act finale.

C.G. This is an extreme case of the 'suspended moment' we talked about earlier. This time the characters are snatched from reality onto Cloud Nine, along with their melting ice-creams, by the extraordinary situation in which they find themselves. It is one of the most magical moments in Rossini's score: it leads into one of his famous *crescendo* ensembles and it is only at the fall of the curtain that everyone is hurled back to Earth. For me, it also sums up the extraordinary treatment Rossini gives this eternal tale: it is a work of genius and gives us all constant pleasure, however often we find ourselves involved with it.

N.J. You and Mark Elder seem to agree on so many points: what about your work with each other on this opera? As this was the third time you have directed the opera (and the fourth year of the production), how did you react to his opinions?

C.G. He is a conductor who is as much concerned with the total dramatic effect as the musical result. Far from resenting what he often would call his interference, I found this collaboration stimulating and rewarding. All too often a conductor turns up at the last moment and seems to be entirely unconcerned with what happens on stage: this is totally frustrating for a director. I know that the 'original' cast members of this production (Della Jones and Meryl Drower) agree with me that Mark's insight and commitment helped us all to build anew and develop an existing production into something fresh and exciting.

M'elle Cinti d'Amoreau, after Grevedon, an early performer of Angelina (Opera Rara Collection)

41

Thematic Guide

Many of the themes from the opera have been identified in the articles by numbers in square brackets, which refer to the themes set out on these pages. The themes are also identified by the numbers in brackets at the corresponding points in the libretto, so that the words can be related to the musical themes.

[1] OVERTURE

Allegro vivace

p leggiero

[2]

[3]

[4] CLORINDA

Allegro con brio

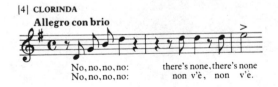

No, no, no, no: there's none, there's none
No, no, no, no: non v'è,   non   v'è.

[5] CINDERELLA (*in a tone of resignation*)

Andantino

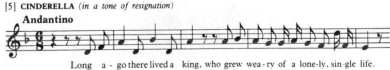

Long   a - go there lived a   king, who grew wea - ry of a lone-ly, sin-gle life.
U - na vol - ta c'era un   re,   che a star so-lo, che a star so-lo s'anno-io;

Allegro con brio

Oh, gra-cious daugh-ters of Don Ma-gni-fi-co, our Prince Ra-mi — ro will soon be here.

O fi-glie_a-ma-bi-li di Don Ma-gni-fi-co, Ramiro_il princi-pe or or ver-rà.

|7| TISBE, CLORINDA

Allegro

T { Cin-der-el-la, here to me. } C { Cin-der-el-la, here to me. }

Ce-ne-ren-to-la vien quà. Ce-ne-ren-to-la vien quà.

|8a| RAMIRO (*to himself*)

Maestoso

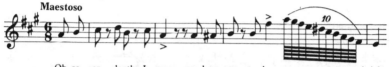

Oh, so ar-dently I gaze on her eyes, so clear, so ——————— bright.

Un so-a-ve non so che in que-gli_oc-chi scin-til ——————— lò.

|8b| DON RAMIRO

She is de-light-ful, she is en — chant — ing all my ————

U-na gra-zia, un cer-to_in — can — to par che ————

sen — ses ——————— now be ——————— guiling

bril — li ——————— su quel ——————— vi-so

|9| DANDINI

Allegro moderato

Like the bee, as he roams o'er the bow ——————— er

Come un' a-pe ne'gior-ni d'a-pri ——————— le

|10| CINDERELLA

Allegro

One hour — all my vi ——————— sions ex-ceed-ing. Oh ——— take me ——— to the ——— ball.

Un' o ——— ra, un'o ——— ra — so —la, por ——— ta — te — mi_a bal ——— lar.

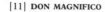

[11] DON MAGNIFICO

Moderato

It's plain e - nough to see   up - on their fa——— ces

Nel volto e - sta - ti - co   di questo e quel——— lo

[12] DON MAGNIFICO

Allegro vivace

If you let   out a word of   a - ny - thing you've heard,

you'll pay the   pe nal ty, you understand?

Se   tu più   mormo - ri   so-lo una   sil - la - ba, un   cimi - te - ri - o   qui si   fa - ra,

[13] RAMIRO

Vivace

sotto voce

Tell me quickly   in a whisper,   while the o — thers can — not   hear us.

Zit - to, zit - to: piano, piano: senza   stre - pi - to e   ru——— mo — re,

[14] CINDERELLA

Maestoso

(Let)   no de - cei ————————————

(For)   tu - na   ca ————————————

————————————— ver   woo   me.

————————————— pric - cio   sa:

[15] CLORINDA

Andante maestoso

I'd   like   to speak   my   feel———— ings,   but words   will   not be   found.

Par - lar   pen sar   vor - re———— i,   par - lar,   pen—— sar   non— so.

44

[16] **SEXTET** *(Finale Act One)*

In a dream, I'm in a gar-den, in a gar-den, in a garden. And a–

Mi par· d'esser, mi par d'esser–e so—gnando fra giardi-ni, fra giar–

– mong the trees a-mong the trees I wan - der.

– di - ni, fra giardi - ni, fra bo -- schetti.

[17] **DON MAGNIFICO'S ARIA**

[18a] **DON RAMIRO**

Yes, I shall find her, I swear it.

Si, ri——— tro——— var——— la io giu———ro.

[18b] **DON RAMIRO, CHORUS**

R { In ev'—ry dwelling, our pur - pose tell-ing, { In ev'—ry dwell-ing our pur-pose tell-ing.
C
{ Noi vo– le— re— mo, do-man - de— re—mo. { Noi vo– le - re— mo, do-man-de— re—mo.

[19] **DANDINI**

You'll be staggered, and as — toun—ded,

Un se – gre – to d'impor– tan - za

Maestoso

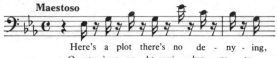

Here's a plot there's no de - ny - ing,
Questo è un no – do avvi— lup —pa — to,

[21] CINDERELLA

Andantino

Ah, my— lord, I — pray ex - cuse me.
Ah si— gnor, s'è — ver che in pet - to

[22] CLORINDA, TISBE

Vivace

Hear them moan and hear them mut -ter.
Quel— lo bron - to — la e bor — bot - ta,

[23a] CINDERELLA

Andante *a piacere*

Born to a life that was lone———ly,
Nac - qui all'a-ffanno e al pian———to,

[23b] CINDERELLA

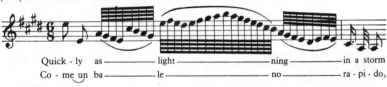

Quick - ly as——— light———ning———in a storm
Co - me un ba——— le——— no——— ra - pi - do,

[23c] CINDERELLA

Allegro

Now no lon - ger by the cin-ders shall I sing my plaintive song, no.
Non più me - sta accanto al fuoco sta—rò so - la a gor-gheg - giar, no.

[23d] CINDERELLA

Like the day——— light,
Ah fuun lam——— po,

La Cenerentola
ossia
La Bontà in Trionfo
(Cinderella or Goodness Triumphant)

Melodramma giocoso in two acts
by Gioachino Rossini

Libretto by Giacomo Ferretti
English translation by Arthur Jacobs

This is the complete Italian libretto written by Ferretti, incorporating his scene descriptions and stage directions. These do not necessarily reflect the current ENO (or any other) production. The Italian text follows old-fashioned spellings and is laid out mainly in rhyming verse. Since the opera is often cut in performance, notes show where scenes are occasionally rearranged. Arthur Jacob's translation was made in 1953 for a television performance and then used in 1959 by Sadler's Wells. Although the performing translation has itself been shortened for English National Opera performances at the London Coliseum, the complete text is reproduced here with the approval of all concerned.

The titles of musical pieces follow the stage directions after an oblique and the numbers in square brackets refer to the thematic guide. The braces in the margin indicate that the characters sing their words together.

La Cenerentola was first performed on January 25, 1817 at the Teatro Valle, in Rome. The first performance in London was at the King's Theatre, Haymarket on January 8, 1820. The first performance in the USA was at the Park Street Theatre, New York on June 27, 1826. It is supposed to have been the first opera produced in Australia (Sydney, February 12, 1844, in English). It was first performed by Sadler's Wells Opera on October 29, 1959 and by English National Opera, in a production originally mounted for English Music Theatre, at the London Coliseum on September 6, 1979.

THE CHARACTERS

Alidoro *philosopher, Don Ramiro's tutor*	bass
Clorinda ⎱ *daughters of Don Magnifico* Tisbe ⎰	soprano mezzo-soprano
Angelina *known as Cinderella, Don Magnifico's* *step-daughter*	contralto
Don Magnifico *baron of Monte Fiascone*	bass-baritone buffo
Don Ramiro *prince of Salerno*	tenor
Dandini *his valet*	bass
Courtiers and Servants of the Prince	tenors, basses

The action takes place partly in an old castle belonging to Don Magnifico, and partly in the Prince's country retreat ('un casino di delizie'), about half a mile away.

Act One

Scene One. *An ancient hall in the Baron's castle, with doors. To the right a fireplace, a little table with a mirror, a basket of flowers, and chairs. Clorinda is practising a 'chassée' (a dance step); Tisbe is adorning herself with a flower, now at her bosom, then on her brow; Cinderella is using bellows at the fireplace to brew a pot of coffee. | Introduction*

CLORINDA [4]

No, no, no, no; there's none, there's none,	No, no, no, no; non v'è, non v'è
None can dance a step so well,	Chi strisciar sappia così
None can dance a step so well.	Leggerissimo *sciassè*.

TISBE

Yes, yes, yes, yes. It suits me so.	Sì, sì, sì, sì; va bene quì . . .
Better so? No, better so.	Meglio quì . . . nò, meglio quì . . .
Which is best it's hard to tell.	Risaltar di più mi fa.

CLORINDA, TISBE

To such beauty, to such art,	A quest'arte, a tal beltà,
Any man must lose his heart.	Sdrucciolar ognun dovrà.

CINDERELLA [5]
(in a resigned tone)

Long ago there lived a king	Una volta c'era un re,
Who grew weary	Che a star solo,
Of a lonely, single life.	Che a star solo s'annoio;
All around he sought a wife,	Cerca, cerca, ritrovò:
But there were three who claimed the ring. So what then?	Ma il volean sposare in tre, cosa fà?
He chose not the rich nor fair,	Sprezzò il fasto, e la beltà,
But the one nobody knew.	E alla fin sceglie per sè
She was modest, she was simple,	L'innocenza, l'innocenza,
She was simple, kind and true.	L'innocenza, e la bontà.
Tra la la la, tra la la la, tra la la la.	Là là là là, lì lì lì lì, là là là là.

CLORINDA, TISBE

Cinderella, will you hold your tongue?	Cenerentola, finiscila
It's that song you're always singing.	Con la solita canzone.
Cinderella, stop that aweful song!	*(repeat)*
Through our heads it's always ringing.	

CINDERELLA

I must work and have no leisure	Presso al fuoco in un cantone
But since I've no other pleasure	*(repeat)*
Surely I may sing my song.	Via lasciatemi cantar.
Long ago there lived a king	[5] Una volta . . . c'era un re,
Long ago . . .	Una volta . . .

CLORINDA, TISBE

Yes, quite long enough.	E due, e tre.

CLORINDA

Long enough we've suffered so.	La finisci, sì, o nò?

49

CLORINDA, TISBE	
Will you finish, yes or no?	Se non taci, ti darò . . .

CINDERELLA [5]

Long ago there . . .	Una volta . . .

There is a knock at the door.

ALL

Who is there at the door?	Chi sarà? Chi sarà?

Cinderella opens the door. Enter Alidoro, dressed as a beggar.

ALIDORO

Noble ladies, I am poor.	Un tantin di carità,
Do not turn me from your door.	*(repeat)*

CLORINDA, TISBE

Off! You beggar, go away.	Accatoni! via di quà.

CINDERELLA
*(pouring out a cup of coffee, and giving it, with some bread, to Alidoro,
so her step-sisters do not see)*

Here's some bread that I've been baking,	Zitto, zitto! su prendete
More I'd gladly see you taking.	Questo pò di colazione.
Oh, alas, that I can never turn	Ah, non reggo alla passione;
Their bitterness away.	Che crudel fatalità!

ALIDORO

Heaven watches o'er us ever,	Forse il Cielo il guiderdone;
Your reward may come today.	Pria di notte vi darà.

CLORINDA, TISBE
(preening themselves)

For a husband rich and clever	Risvegliar dolce passione
I know just the trick to play.	Più di me nessuna sa.

CLORINDA
(noticing that Alidoro is still there)

What, you rascal, are you still there?	Ma che vedo? . . . Ancora lì!

TISBE

And drinking coffee, and eating too?	Anche un pane? del caffè?

CLORINDA
(turning on Cinderella)

What a wicked thing to do!	Prendi, questo viene a te.

CINDERELLA
(interposing)

Oh, will no one take my part?	Ah! soccorso chi mi da?

ALIDORO

Have some pity in your heart.	Vi fermate per pietà!

Enter Courtiers, dressed for riding.

COURTIERS [6]

Oh, gracious daughters of Don Magnifico,	O figlie amabili di don Magnifico

50

Our Prince Ramiro will soon be here.	Ramiro il principe or or verrà;
And to his palace he'll bid you come,	Al suo palagio vi condurrà!
To dance and sup with royal cheer.	Si canterà, si danzerà;
Then from the company he'll pick the fairest one.	Poi la bellissima fra l'altre femmine
Yes, she, the rarest one, shall be his bride.	Sposa carissima per lui sarà.

CLORINDA

The Prince himself, you say?	Ma dunque il principe . . .

COURTIERS

Soon at your side —	Or or verrà.

CLORINDA, TISBE, CINDERELLA

And then the fairest one?	E la bellissima . . .

COURTIERS

— Shall be his bride.	Si sceglierà.

TISBE, CLORINDA [7]

Cinderella, here to me.	Cenerentola vien quà;
Bring my bonnet, bring my shawl.	Le mie scarpe, il mio bonne.
Bring my hat with feathers tall.	Le mie piume, il mio colliè.
I'm already so excited	Nel cervello ho una fucina
What a conquest now for me.	Son più bella, e vo' trionfar.
Just a smile and we are plighted,	A un sorriso, a un'occhiattina
And a princess I shall be.	Don Ramiro ha da cascar.

CINDERELLA

Cinderella, bring my hat	Cenerentola vien quà,
Cinderella this and that.	Cenerentola va là,
Cinderella, bring my shawl.	Cenerentola va su,
Always at their beck and call.	Cenerentola va giù . . .
I must work without an ending,	Questo e proprio uno strapazzo!
Always working, never free.	Mi volete far crepar?
While the others, merry-making,	Chi alla festa, chi al solazzo:
Never think of taking me.	Ed io resto qui a soffiar.

ALIDORO

Though they're getting so excited,	Nel cervello una fucina
Silly girls as I can see,	Sta le pazze a martellar;
When the wrong will soon be righted,	Ma già pronta è la ruina
What a laughing-stock they'll be.	Voglio ridere, e schiattar.

COURTIERS

They are getting so excited,	Già nel capo una fucina
Silly girls, as we can see,	Sta le donne a martellar;
To the great event invited	Il cimento s'avvicina,
For the Prince's bride-to-be.	Il gran punto di trionfar.

Recitative and Cavatina

CLORINDA

(to Cinderella, giving her money for the Courtiers, who retire)

Give them this money. Thank you!	Date lor mezzo scudo. Grazie. Ai cenni
Kindly tell his Highness we've accepted.	Del Principe noi siamo.

(to Alidoro)

Still here, you beggar?	Ancor qui siete?

51

It smells here! Be off, now.
If you don't, you'll be sorry.

Qual tanfo! andate, o ve ne pentirete.

CINDERELLA
(to Alidoro)

That money that I gave them
I wish I could have giv'n you,
But I haven't a farthing. I am so sorry.

I would give anything if I thought I
could help you.

Io poi quel mezzo scudo
A voi l'avrei donato;
Ma non ho mezzo soldo. (Il core in
mezzo

Mi spaccherei per darlo a un infelice).

ALIDORO
(as he leaves, to Cinderella)

Before tomorrow's gone, you may be
happy.

(Forse al novello dì sarai felice.)

Exit Alidoro.

TISBE

But we've no time to be dawdling.

Ma non v'è tempo da perdere.

CLORINDA

Don't you think we should go and tell
father?

Nostro padre
Avvisarne convien.

TISBE
(contending who should go first)

My dear Clorinda,
Pray allow me to tell him.

Esser la prima
Voglio a darne la nuova.

CLORINDA

My dearest Tisbe,
Remember I'm the elder.

Oh! mi perdoni,
Io sono la maggiore.

TISBE

No, no, I'll go and tell him.

No no, gliel vo'dir io.

CLORINDA

No, no it is my duty.
I'll wake him at once: then you can
follow.

È questo il dover mio.
Io svegliar lo vuo! Venite appresso.

TISBE

All right, for once I'll let you.

Oh! non la vincerai.

CLORINDA

Wait now . . . he's coming.

Ecco egli stesso.

Don Magnifico enters, in a bad temper, in his nightcap and dressing gown.

DON MAGNIFICO

Why the devil did I get you as my
offspring?
I detest you, I renounce you.
Such a dream that I was dreaming
Till you roused me from my bed

Miei rampolli, miei rampolli femminini

Vi ripudio; mi vergogno!
Un magnifico mio sogno
Mi veniste a sconcertar.

(refusing them his hand to kiss)
With a noise to wake the dead!

(repeat)

52

(Clorinda and Tisbe laughing when not observed)

Interrupting all my dreaming,
With your chattering and screaming!
Now attend your noble father,
Pause and ponder on my dream.
In this dream I was no baron,
Not a regal and sedate one,
I was turned into a donkey —
Yes, a donkey, but a great one.
Quick as lightning, and rather fright'ning
I grew feathers, I could spot them,
Though most donkeys haven't got them.
So as graceful as a seagull
And as powerful as an eagle,
Up on high, whoosh!, I flew.
To the summit of a steeple
In a moment I had flown,
And I sat atop the belfry
Like a monarch on a throne.
Then I listened while below me
All the bells began their song.
Ding, dong, ding, dong.
When your silly chitter-chatter
Came and woke me with a fright,
And the dream was lost for ever
Gone for ever from my sight.
And your bickering, bickering, bickering
Went on and on like any pair of dogs
      before a fight.
Yet despite your lack of manners
You shall hear the revelation,
For a dream must have a meaning,
So behold my explanation.
All that chiming of the bells,
A happy wedding it foretells.
And the feathers? You, my daughters.
And the flying? High promotion.
Yes, but what about the donkey?
Why, the donkey, it was I . . .
For I'm certain, when I see you,
That an ass was your papa.
Each of you shall marry princes,
And your children kings shall be;
And a dozen royal babies
I shall dandle on my knee.
With a little monarch there.
Hip hooray, the king's advancing
And a baby monarch there,
Up and down the nursery prancing.
What a family I can see,
And what a glory there for me!
With his Majesty here and his Majesty
      there,
And his Majesty perched on a nursery
      chair.
See his Majesty go and his Majesty come,
And his Majesty sucking his Majesty's
      thumb.

Come son mortificate!
Degne figlie d'un Barone!
Via: silenzio, ed attenzione,
State il sogno a meditar.
Mi sognai tra il fosco, e il chiaro
(repeat)
Un bellissimo somaro;
Un somaro, ma solenne.
Quando a un tratto, oh che portento!
Sulle spalle a cento a cento
(repeat)
Gli spuntavano le penne,
(repeat)
Ed in alto, sen, volò!
Ed in cima a un campanile
Come in trono si fermò
(repeat)

Si sentiano per di sotto
Le campanne a sdindonar . . .
Din, don, din, don.
Col ci, ci, ci, ci di botto
Mi faceste risvegliar.
(repeat)

Ma d'un sogno sì intralciato
Ecco il simbolo spiegato.
(repeat)

La campana suona a festa?
Allegria in casa mia.
Quelle penne? Siete voi:
Quel gran volo? Plebe addio.
Resta l'asino di poi?
Ma quell'asino son io,
Chi vi guarda vede chiaro
Che il somaro è il genitor.
Fertilissima Regina
L'una, e l'altra diverrà,
Ed il nonno una dozzina
Di nepoti abbraccierà.
Un re piccolo di quà . . .
Servo , servo, servo, servo;
Un re bambolo di là . . .
E la gloria mia sarà.
(repeat)

Un re piccolo di quà.

(repeat)

I shall love it, I can see, And what a glory there for me, just for me.	E la gloria mia sarà. (repeat)

Recitative

CLORINDA
(interrupting each other)

D'you know that any moment . . .	Sappiate che fra poco . . .

TISBE

D'you know that Prince Ramiro . . .	Il Principe Ramiro . . .

CLORINDA

Now for three days he's been living near us . . .	Che son tre dì, che nella deliziosa . . .

TISBE

It's about half a mile off, The palace where he's staying . . .	Vicino mezzo miglio Venuto è ad abitar . . .

CLORINDA

He's to choose Sceglie una sposa . . . a bride . . .	

TISBE

And we've had an invitation . . .	Ci mandò ad invitar . . .

CLORINDA

And very shortly . . . E fra momenti . . .	

TISBE

He will be here to call for us . . .	Arriverà per prenderci . . .

CLORINDA

And the fairest one, E la scelta He will make her his bride.	La più bella sarà.

DON MAGNIFICO
(with an air of wonder and amazement)

Really, d'you say so?	Figlie, che dite?
This mighty Prince (even though I've not met him)	Quel Principon! Quantunque io nol conosca . . .
He's to choose, he's to wed, and you're invited!	Sceglierà . . . v'invitò . . . sposa . . . più bella!
I'm feeling rather dizzy.	Io cado in svenimento.
Cinderella, come quickly,	Cenerentola, presto,
Bring me a strong cup of coffee. But this is awful,	Portami il mio caffè. Viscere mie,
Half of my precious mansion is in ruins, the rest on the verge.	Metà del mio palazzo è già crollata, e l'altra e in agonia.
There's not much for it. We'll do the best we can, though.	Fatevi onore, mettiamoci un puntello.
You two, try and talk sensibly.	Figlie state in vervello,
Be sure to mind your manners, for heaven's sake!	Parlate in punto, e virgola,

He paces up and down, and brings them back as they are about to leave.

Dress as befits your title.	Per carità: pensate ad abbigliarvi:
In this sort of campaign the first shot's vital.	Si tratta niente men che imprinciparvi.

Exeunt. Enter Don Ramiro, dressed as a squire. He looks around him and advances cautiously.
/Scena and Duet

RAMIRO

The place is deserted. Hello, there!   Tutto è deserto. Amici?
Can no-one hear me? Unsuspected,   Nessun risponde. In questa
In disguise as a servant,   Simulata sembianza . . .
The ladies I shall observe. Is no one   Le belle osserverò. Nè viene alcuno? . . .
   coming?
But yet I'm told to hope   Eppur mi diè speranza
By my wise Alidoro,   Il sapiente Alidoro,
That here, gracious, full of virtue,   Che quì saggia, e vezzosa
Worthy to share my throne, my bride   Degna di me trovar saprò la sposa.
   awaits me.
To marry — but not for love! Ah . . .   Sposarsi, e non amar! Legge tiranna,
   wretched fate . . .
By command of my father, whether I   Che nel fior de' miei giorni
   love or no, I must marry!   A difficile scelta mi condanna!
Ah well, I wonder . . .   Cerchiam, vediamo.

Cinderella returns, singing to herself and abstracted in thought, carrying a coffee cup and saucer.

CINDERELLA [5]

Long ago there lived a . . .   Una volta c'era . . .
            (everything falls from her hand)

RAMIRO

What's the matter?   Che cos'è?

CINDERELLA

      Oh, how my heart beats!   Che batticuore!

RAMIRO

Do you think I'm a monster?   Forse un mostro son'io?

CINDERELLA
(taken aback, then recovering herself)
            Yes . . . no . . .   Sì . . . no, Signore.
forgive me . . .

RAMIRO
(to himself) [8a]
Oh, so ardently I gaze   Un soave non so che
On her eyes, so clear, so bright.   In quegli occhi scintillò.

CINDERELLA
(to herself)
How enchanting are his ways,   Io vorrei saper perchè
I am filled with strange delight.   Il mio cor mi palpitò.

RAMIRO

Could I tell her? Oh, no, I dare not.   Le direi, ma non ardisco.

CINDERELLA

Can I tell him, oh no, I may not,   Parlar voglio, e taccio intanto.
I must keep silent.

CINDERELLA, RAMIRO [8b]

(She) is delightful. (She) is enchanting   Una grazia, un certo incanto
(He)   (He)

55

All my senses now beguiling.   Par che brilli su quel viso.

Ah, how sweetly now (she's)(he's) smiling: Quanto caro è quel sorriso!

All my desire I may hope to gain.   Scende all'alma, e fa sperar.

RAMIRO

I'm awaiting the baron's daughters.   Del Barone le figlie io chiedo.

Pray, where are they? For no-one's answered.   Dove son? quì non le vedo.

CINDERELLA

They are in the other rooms, sir,   Stan di là nell'altre stanze.

And must not have heard your knocking.

Soon they'll be here. (My hopes are dying).   Or verranno. (Addio speranze.)

RAMIRO
(with interest)

But, excuse me, who may you be?   Ma di grazia, voi chi siete?

CINDERELLA

Who may I be? Why, I don't know.   Io chi sono? Eh non lo sò.

RAMIRO

You don't know?   Nol sapete?

CINDERELLA

No, not really.   Quasi no.

RAMIRO

Can't you tell me?   Nol sapete?

CINDERELLA
(rapidly correcting herself and getting muddled)

Well, I'll try.   Quasi no.

Father isn't really father   Quel ch'e padre, non e padre . . .

And the girls are not my sisters,   Onde poi le due sorelle . . .

For a widow was my mother,   Era vedova mia madre . . .

Lost her husband, wed another.   Ma fu madre ancor di quelle . . .

So he isn't really father . . .   Questo padre pien d' orgoglio . . .

I am getting in a muddle.   Sta a vedere che m'imbroglio.

Ah, forgive me, sir, I pray you . . .   Deh scusate, perdonate

I am as lost as I can be.   Alla mia semplicità.

RAMIRO

How delightful, how enchanting   Mi seduce, m'innamora

Are the blushes I can see.   Quella sua semplicità.

CLORINDA, TISBE
(offstage)

Cinderella! Come here!   Cenerentola da me!

RAMIRO

Who is making all that noise?   Quante voci, che cos'è?

CINDERELLA

Not a moment will they leave me.   A ponente, ed a levante,

Always something more to grieve me.   A sirocco, a tramontana,

With my labour I am laden   Non ho calma un solo istante.

Ev'ry day and ev'ry hour.	Tutto, tutto tocca a me.
And now goodbye, sir,	Vengo, vengo. Addio signore!
If you'll excuse me. Coming! Coming!	*(repeat)*

(running first towards one door, and then to the other)

(Oh, alas, I must be going,	(Ah! ci lascio proprio il core:
	(with feeling)
Yet with him I leave my heart.)	Questo cor più mio non è.)

RAMIRO
(rapt, always looking at Cinderella)

With a modesty so charming	Quell'accento, quel sembiante
And a manner so disarming,	È una cosa sovrumana.
This demure and lovely maiden	Io mi perdo in questo istante:
Has me gladly in her power.	Già più me non trovo in me.
Oh, how charming, how disarming.	Che innocenza! che candore!
She has won my love for ever,	Ah! m'invola proprio il core:
Yet alas we're torn apart.	Questo cor più mio non è.

CINDERELLA, RAMIRO

Journeys end in lovers' meeting,	Ah! (ci lascio) proprio il core:
That's a saying worth repeating.	(m'invola)
But today our joy is fleeting;	*(repeat)*
From each other we must part.	Questo cor più mio non è.

Exit Cinderella. | Recitative

RAMIRO

I find it strange that in such rags and tatters	Non so che dir. Come in sì rozze spoglie
Such loveliness should be. But Don Magnifico	Un volto sì gentil! Ma don Magnifico
Has still not shown his face. He does not know me.	Non apparisce ancor. Nunziar vorrei
I'll say I am the Prince's squire and servant.	Del mascherato principe l'arrivo.
My disguise will protect me.	Fortunato consiglio!
Dressed like a simple courtier,	Da semplice scudiero
No one will notice me, and I	Il cuore delle femmine
Can watch the ladies well. Meanwhile Dandini	Meglio svelar saprò. Dandini intanto
Will amuse himself in my part . . .	Recitando da principe . . .

Enter Don Magnifico.

DON MAGNIFICO

Oh, sir,	Domando
I've kept you waiting, pray excuse me.	Un milion di perdoni.
Tell me, when shall we greet his Highness?	Dica: Sua Altezza il Prence . . .

RAMIRO

He's on his way here.	Or or arriva.

DON MAGNIFICO

Then shortly?	E quando?

RAMIRO

Say in five minutes.	Fra tre minuti.

In five minutes!   Tre minuti! ah figlie!
My girls are not ready yet.   Sbrigatevi:
                    (calling)
            Make haste, there!   che serve?
I'd better go and stir them. Excuse me,   Le vado ad affettar. Scusi: con queste
It's not that they're wasting time in   Ragazze benedette
   prattle.
They're loading ammunition before the   Un secolo è un momento alla toeletta.
   battle.

Exit Don Magnifico.

What a donkey! Yet Alidoro, my adviser,   Che buffone! e Alidoro mio maestro
Says kindness, truth and virtue   Sostien che in queste mura
Are found within this dwelling.   Sta la bontà più pura.
Patience, patience, we'll see. In just a   Basta, basta vedrem. Alle sue figlie
   moment
I'll meet the Baron's daughters.   ⸠ Convien che m' avvicini . . .
But who's that? Yes, I thought so.   Qualfragor . . . non m'inganno, ecco
Here comes Dandini.   Dandini.

Enter Dandini with Courtiers; Don Magnifico, Clorinda and Tisbe. | Chorus and Cavatina

This is the day when presently   Scegli la sposa, affrettati:
Our Prince shall choose a bride.   Sen vola via l'età:
Mother of princes she shall be,   La principesca linea
And Queen of all beside.   Se no, s'estinguerà.

Like the bee, as he roams o'er the bower, Come un'ape ne' giorni d'aprile
Now to rose, now to lily a-straying.   Va volando leggiera, e scherzosa;
All the summer his fancy is playing,   Corre al giglio, poi salta alla rosa,
Seeking always the one sweetest flower—   Dolce un fiore a cercare per se;
So I wander from maiden to maiden,   Tra le belle m'aggiro, e rimiro:
And have marvelled at many a fair one.   Ne ho veduto già tante, e poi tante,
Ah, but never a sufficiently rare one   Ma non trovo un giudizio, un sembiante
Have I found where my wings I could   Un boccone squisito per me.
   rest,
Where at last there's an end to my quest. *(repeat)*

Clorinda and Tisbe come forward, and are presented to Dandini by Don Magnifico.

Highness . . .   Prence . . .

Highness . . .   Sire . . .

          Your Highness,   Ma quanti favori!
so gracious!

We're all quite overwhelmed by the   Che diluvio, che abisso di onori.
   honour.

DANDINI
(first to one, then the other)

Thank you, you are welcome.	Nulla, nulla. Vezzosa! graziosa!
How charming! vivacious!	

(aside to Ramiro; then to Don Magnifico)

(I pretended. Aren't I splendid?)	(Dico bene?) Son tutte papà.
Yes, really, it's true.	*(repeat)*
They're exactly like you.	

RAMIRO

(Steady, a joke can be carried too far!	(Bestia! attento, ti scosta, va là.)
Steady, remember how simple they are.)	*(repeat)*

DANDINI
(to the sisters, who are eyeing him passionately)

Ah, have pity, oh, spare those fatal glances,	Per pietà quelle ciglia abbassate.
Lest I die in an ecstasy of anguish,	
For already before you I languish.	Galloppando sen va la ragione
My defences you've shattered apart.	E fra i colpi d'un doppio cannone
Ah, why cause me this exquisite rapture?	Spalancata la brecchia è di già.
Ah, release me, disarmed by Cupid's dart.	*(repeat)*
At your feet, ah, behold here your capture,	
Ah, have pity on my heart.	
Such beauty! No wonder, with such a papa!	Vezzosa! graziosa! son tutte papà.
(Oh, how easy I find them to flatter,	(Ma al finir della nostra commedia
For the three of them haven't a brain.	Che tragedia quì nascer dovrà!)
They give ear to all my stupidest patter,	*(repeat)*
And I trick them again and again!	
How delightedly all of them chatter	
At the prize that they think to obtain.	
But if they knew the truth of the matter	
Then their pleasure would turn into pain.)	

TISBE, CLORINDA

See what longing he shows in his glances	(Ei mi guarda, sospira, delira,
I have captured the prize, it is plain.	Non v'è dubbio è mio schiavo di già.)
(repeat)	*(repeat)*

RAMIRO

Shall I see her again, my enchantress,	Ah! perchè qui non viene colei
Or will all expectation be vain?	Con quell'aria di grazia, e bontà?

DON MAGNIFICO

They will soon start to call me your Highness —	(È già cotto, stracotto, spolpato,
That's the title that I shall obtain.	L'Eccellenza divien Maestà.)

CHORUS

This is a day of happiness	Scegli la sposa, affrettati,
When he his bride shall gain.	Sen vola via l'eta.

Recitative and Quintet

DANDINI
(observing Clorinda, Tisbe and Don Magnifico)

Again I compliment you! What fine figures,	Allegrissimamente, che bei quadri!

English	Italian
What an eyelash! What eyes too!	Che bocchino! che ciglia!
Who would have thought it? But seeing is believing.	Siete l'ottava, e nona meraviglia;
This shows the virtue of heredity.	Già *talem Patrem, tales Filias.*

CLORINDA
(curtseying)

Thank you.	Grazie!

DON MAGNIFICO
(bowing)

Oh, most exalted Highness,	Altezza delle Altezze
What honour. I've no words left. I'm speechless.	Che dice? mi confonde: debolezze.

DANDINI

They're good enough for statues.	Vere figure etrusche.

(aside to Ramiro)

(Aren't I splendid?)	(Dico bene?)

RAMIRO
(aside to Dandini)

(I think you overdo it.)	(Cominci a dirle grosse.)

DANDINI
(aside to Ramiro)

(No, it's what they're expecting. It's the grand manner	(Io recito da grande, e grande essendo,
A prince is meant to have.)	Grandi le ho da sparar.)

DON MAGNIFICO
(aside to his daughters with self-satisfaction)

(Now there's a prince for you.	(Bel Principotto!
He shan't escape, I promise.)	Che non vi fugga: attente.)

DANDINI

And now may I continue to inform you	Or dunque seguitando quel discorso
What I had not related.	Che non ho cominciato,
I came home from travels, educated,	Dai miei lunghi viaggi ritornato,
And then my ageing father stated	E il mio papà trovato,
That our fam'ly must be perpetuated.	Che fra i quondam è capitombolato,
So a law he had promulgated,	E spirando ha ordinato
That unless I got mated,	Che a vista qual cambiale io sia sposato,
I'd lose the fortune that I'd anticipated.	O son diseredato;
So you are welcome, as I have intimated,	Fatto ho un invito a tutto il vincinato,
To the ball where from the beauties celebrated,	E trovando un boccone delicato,
I'll pick the lucky-fated.	Per me l'ho destinato;
I trust that your mind now is quite illuminated.	Ho detto, ho detto, e adesso prendo fiato.

DON MAGNIFICO
(astonished)

(What eloquence, what manners!)	(Che eloquenza sublime!)

CINDERELLA
(comparing Dandini with Ramiro, who is watching her)

(Oh, how well-dressed he looks!	(Ih! che bell'abito!
And there's the one I spoke to.)	E quell'altro mi guarda.)

RAMIRO

(Again I see her.   (Ecco colei!
How beautiful she is.)   Come palpita il cor.)

DANDINI

Most noble ladies,   Belle ragazze,
If you will kindly accept now as your   Se volete onorar del vostro braccio
   escorts
These gentlemen who serve me, the   I nostri Cavalieri, il legno è pronto.
   coach is ready.

CLORINDA

With pleasure.   Andiam.

TISBE

Papa, and your Highness, pray come to   Papà, Eccellenza, non tardate a venir
   join us soon.

Exeunt Clorinda and Tisbe with the Courtiers.

DON MAGNIFICO
(to Cinderella)

You run along.   Che fai tu qui?
Get my hat and cane this minute.   Il cappello, e il bastone.

CINDERELLA
(leaving)

Oh, yes, at once.   Eh! Signor sì.

DANDINI

Pray, sir, do me the honour   Perseguitate, presto
Of gracing my palace   Con i piè baronali
With your baronial and glorious presence.   I magnifici miei quarti reali.

Exit Dandini.

DON MAGNIFICO
(entering the room into which Cinderella went)

Enter your carriage, I'll follow.   Monti in carrozza, e vengo.

RAMIRO

(If I stay here,   (Èppur colei
I may see her again.)   Vò riveder.)

DON MAGNIFICO
(off stage, angrily)

Don't bother me.   Ma lasciami.

RAMIRO

(He's angry).   (La sgrida?)

CINDERELLA
(returning)

Oh, please, sir!   Sentite.

DON MAGNIFICO
(returns with hat and stick)

Some other time, then.   Il tempo vola.

RAMIRO

(What a brute!)   (Che vorrà?)

DON MAGNIFICO

Will you stop it?   Vuoi lasciarmi?

CINDERELLA

Only a word, sir.   Una parola.
Tonight . . . oh, do not turn away my   Signor, una parola:
  pleading,
Tonight give me an hour of happiness,   In casa di quel Principe
One hour, all my visions exceeding.   [10]   Un'ora, un'ora sola,
Oh, take me to the ball.   Portatemi a ballar.

DON MAGNIFICO

Ha, ha! Yes, you'd be wonderful,   Ih! ih! La bella Venere!
So pretty, such a figure.   Vezzosa! pomposetta!
Get back there to your scullery.   Sguajata! covacenere!
Off with you! Let me go!   Lasciami, deggio andar.
A bride-to-be! From the scullery!   (repeat)

DANDINI
(returning to see Ramiro standing motionless)

What's this? Why are you standing   Cos'è? qui fa la statua?
there?

RAMIRO
(to Dandini)

Be quiet, this needs observing.   Silenzio, ed osserviamo.

DANDINI

But surely we should be going?   Ma andiamo, o non andiamo?

RAMIRO

My heart commands me stay.   Mi sento lacerar.

CINDERELLA

For just a half-hour . . . a quarter . . .   Ma una mezz'ora . . . un quarto . . .

DON MAGNIFICO
(to Cinderella, brandishing his stick menacingly)

Be off, or you'll be worse for it.   Ma lasciami, o ti stritolo.

RAMIRO, DANDINI
(to Don Magnifico)

Have patience.   Fermate.

DON MAGNIFICO
(bowing respectfully to Dandini)

Noble Highness!   Serenissima! . . .
(Get out of here!) Sir, you'll pardon me,   (Ma vattene . . .) Altezzissima! . . .
Such trouble servants give today.   Servaccia ignorantissima!
You can't get good ones anywhere.   (repeat)

RAMIRO, DANDINI

Servant?   Serva?

CINDERELLA

That is —   Cioè . . .

62

DON MAGNIFICO

You hold your tongue!

Her cradle was the scullery.	Vilissima,
She aims at airs and graces,	D'un estrazion bassissima,
And jewels, and fine laces.	Vuol far la sufficiente,
I'll show her what her place is!	La cara, l'avvenente,
Go in at once, go in at once	E non è buona a niente.
And back to work again.	Va in camera, va in camera
	La polvere a spazzar.

RAMIRO

(My anger at his cruelty	(Or ora la mia collera
I hardly can restrain.)	Non posso più frenar.)

DANDINI
(in an authoritative tone)

I pray you, Don Magnifico,	Ma, caro don Magnifico,
From harshness to refrain.	Via non la strapazzar.

CINDERELLA
(with ingenuous expression)

Ah, lonely by the fireside	Ah! sempre fra la cenere
Must I tonight remain?	Sempre dovrò restar?
One hour all my joys exceeding,	Signor; persuadetelo,
Ah, help me now to gain.	Portatemi a ballar,
Must I remain here all alone?	Star sempre fra la cenere?

Enter Alidoro, bearing a register open in his hand, at the moment when Don Magnifico breaks away from Dandini.

ALIDORO

See in this register	Qui nel mio codice
Words plainly telling,	Delle zitelle,
Three sisters there should be	Con don Magnifico
Here in this dwelling.	Stan tre sorelle;
Now must his Highness see	Or che va il Principe
In their variety,	La sposa a scegliere,
All girls and women	*(repeat)*
Throughout all society.	
So with these daughters,	La terza figlia
Call now the third one.	Io vi domando.

DON MAGNIFICO
(confused)

This is a jest, sir,	Che terza figlia
And an absurd one. What other?	Mi va figliando? Che terza . . .

ALIDORO

Your other daughter . . .	Terza sorella . . .

DON MAGNIFICO
(alarmed)

Yes, but . . . she died.	Ella . . . morì.

ALIDORO

Not in this register,	Eppur nel codice
Pray look inside.	Non v'è così.

CINDERELLA
(naively interposing)

(Ah, dare I speak to them?)	(Ah! di me parlano: . . .)
No, she's alive.	No, non mori.

DON MAGNIFICO
(thrusting her into a corner)

Now if you want to go on living	Sta zitta lì.
Shut your mouth and hold your breath.	*(repeat)*
Say not a word.	Guardate quì!
You must conceal it,	Se tu respiri,
If you reveal it,	*(repeat)*
You'll meet your death.	Ti scanno quì.

RAMIRO

Sir, your reply?	Ella morì?

DANDINI

Then did she die?	Ella morì.

DON MAGNIFICO

Your Highness, she died.	Altezza, morì.

DON MAGNIFICO, CINDERELLA, DANDINI, RAMIRO, ALIDORO
(looking at each other)

It's plain enough to see	[11] Nel volto estatico
Upon their faces,	Di questo, e quello,
That guile and perfidy,	Si legge il vortice
Have left their traces,	Del lor cervello,
And in perplexity	Che ondeggia e dubita,
All of them stand. Behold them stand!	E incerto stà.

DON MAGNIFICO

If you let out a word	[12] Se tu più mormori
Of anything you've heard,	Solo una sillaba,
You'll pay the penalty,	Un cimiterio
You understand?	Qui si farà.

CINDERELLA

Don't let him bully me,	Deh soccorretemi,
Oh, did you ever see	Deh non lasciatemi,
A more unhappy girl	Ah! di me misera
In all the land?	Che mai sarà?

ALIDORO

Silence, I beg of you,	Via, meno strepito:
This noise will never do.	Fate silenzio,
Prince, 'tis on your behalf	O qualche scandalo
This I command.	Qui nascerà.

RAMIRO

There is no need to fear,	Via consolatevi:
So long as I am here,	Signor, lasciatela.
I'll see that to you	(Già la mia furia
None shall raise his hand.	Crescendo va.)

DANDINI

Am I a prince indeed,	Io sono un Principe,
Or will you pay no heed?	O sono un cavolo?

Your full obedience   Vi mando al diavolo,
I now demand.   Venite quà.

Dandini forces Don Magnifico to release Cinderella. All follow Dandini. Cinderella runs to her room. Enter Alidoro disguised as a pilgrim. | Recitative

ALIDORO

Beauty, grace, and elegance you'll find Grazie, vezzi, beltà potrai scontrare
At ev'ry corner. But goodness and virtue Ad ogni passo; ma bontà, innocenza,
May still escape you, though you search a Se non si cerca, non si trova mai.
 lifetime.
That's how the world is . . . Daughter! Gran ruota è il mondo . . . Figlia?

CINDERELLA

Daughter! You call me daughter? You're Figlia voi mi chiamate? Oh questa è
 very kind, sir,   bella!
But the Baron's so haughty,   Il padrigno barone
He won't be called my father. But   Non vuole essermi padre, e voi . . .
 you . . .

ALIDORO

Get ready. We must be going.   Tacete: venite meco.

CINDERELLA

Get ready?   E dove?

ALIDORO

It's about time   Or or un cocchio
For the coach to arrive. We'll go in it S'appresserà. Del Principe
To Prince Ramiro's banquet.   Andremo al festino.

CINDERELLA

What, dressed as we are? In fancy dress Con questi stracci? Come Paris e Vienna?
 as beggars?

ALIDORO
(throwing off his disguise to reveal his dress as the Prince's tutor)
Say nothing. Just for this evening   Osservate. Silenzio. Abiti, gioje,
You'll have all you desire: richest of Tutto avrete da me. Fasto, ricchezza
 jewels
And a beautiful gown. You'll be a lady, Non v'abbaglino il cor. Dama sarete;
But don't reveal your secret. In all your Scoprirvi non dovrete. Amor soltanto
 actions
Your heart must be your guide.   Tutto v'insegnerà.

CINDERELLA

Can I be dreaming,   Ma questa è storia;
Or is this a play we're acting?   Oppur una commedia?

ALIDORO

Yes, my daughter,   Figlia mia,
All the world's a stage,   L'allegrezza e la pena
And all the men and women   Son'commedia, e tragedia,
Merely players.   E il mondo è scena.

Music for an aria entitled *'Vasto teatro è il mondo'* to follow this recitative was written by Agolini for the first performance and is still included in the Ricordi vocal score. An alternative scene with recitative and aria was composed by Rossini himself, to

new words, for a production in 1821, when a different singer was engaged; it is reproduced here.

ALIDORO

Yes, ev'rything will change,	Sì, tutto cangerà
And proud presumption	Quel folle orgoglio
Shall decay into dust,	Poca polve sarà
Blown by the breezes;	Gioco del vento;
While tears and lamentation	E al tenero lamento
Will quickly turn into laughter.	Succederà il sorriso.
Daughter . . . daughter . . .	Figlia . . . figlia . . .

CINDERELLA

And do you call me daughter? Oh, yes, I see it;	Figlia voi mi chiamate? O questa è bella!
While my stepfather shuns me and refuses to own me,	Il padrigno Barone non vuol essermi padre
Yet you, a beggar, in all your rags and tatters — as shabby as mine —	E vuoi per altro guardando i stracci vostri — e i stracci miei —
You're a suitable father for such a daughter!	Degna d'un padre tal figlia sarei!

ALIDORO

Hush, my daughter, we must be going.	Taci, figlia, e vieni meco.

CINDERELLA

Going? but where?	Teco; e dove?

ALIDORO

To Prince Ramiro's banquet.	Del Principe al festino.

CINDERELLA

How can you be so cruel?	Ma dimmi, Pellegrino,
Because I gave you only bread and coffee,	Perchè t'ho data poca colazione
Must you mock me and tease me?	Tu mi vieni a burlar?
Be gone, pray! — yes, leave me!	Va via . . . va via!
I must lock the doors	Voglio serrar la porta . . .
To guard against intruders,	Possono entrar de'ladri
Who might — who might —	E allora . . . allora
Who might employ some deception.	Starei fresca d'avvero.

ALIDORO

No! Put such thoughts aside!	No! Sublima il pensiero!
Gone is the life you led!	Tutto cangiò per te!
On paths exalted,	Calpesterai men che
You shall rise above riches,	Fango i tesori,
Making all hearts your capture.	Rapirai tutti i cuori.
So come now, and have no fear.	Vien meco e non temer:
I feel the presence of heav'n above us,	Per te dal l'Alto m'ispira un nume
Of Him whose throne no pow'r can sunder —	A cui non crolla il trono.
And if still you should doubt	E se dubiti ancor
Look, then, and wonder!	Mira chi sono!

(He throws off his cloak, to reveal his proper clothes beneath.)

There on high, 'mid the stars in their splendour,	Là del ciel nell'arcano profondo,
On a throne which endures through the ages,	Del poter sull'altissimo Trono
Reigns our Father, our shield and defender,	Veglia nume signore del mondo,

Whom the tempest obeys in its rages.	Al cui piè basso mormora il tuono.
Knowing all, loving all, he will never	Tutto sa tutto vede e non lascia
Leave his children remote from his love,	Nell'ambascia perir la bontà.
No, no, he redeems then with grace	*(repeat)*
from above	
Though by ashes and weeping surrounded	Fra la cenere, il pianto, l'affanno
From His throne he looks down and	Ei ti vede o fanciulla innocente,
beholds you,	
And as champion of right and of goodness	E cangiando il tuo stato tiranno
With his strength and compassion	Fra l'orror vibra un lampo innocente,
enfolds you.	
So arise, and have no fear.	No, no, no, no, non temer.
All your fortune will alter,	Si è cambiata la scena:
Do not falter but live life anew.	La tua pena cangiando già va.
Have no fear. Be strong, be true.	*(repeat)*
Do you hear a sound approaching,	Un crescente mormorio
Ever louder to the ear?	Non ti sembra d'ascoltar . . .
Then be joyful, it is my carriage	Ah sta lieta: il cocchio mio
Which will take you away from here.	Su cui voli a trionfar!
You look doubtful and unsteady —	Tu mi guardi, ti confondi . . .
Come, young lady, say you're ready!	Ehi, ragazza, non rispondi?
No, your head is in commotion	Sconcertata è la tua testa
All upset by fear and doubt.	E rimbalza qua e là
Like a ship upon the ocean,	Come nave in gran tempesta
Up and down and round about.	Che di sotto in su sen va.
But the cloud has now departed	Ma già il nembo e terminato
And we greet the shining sun.	Scintillò serenità.
For the kindly, for the true and tender-hearted,	Il destino, il destino s'è cangiato
Days of gladness, days of gladness have begun.	L'innocenza, l'innocenza brillerà.

Scene Two: *A room in the palace of Don Ramiro. Enter Dandini in conversation with Don Magnifico, and Clorinda and Tisbe on either arm. Also Ramiro. | Recitative*

DANDINI

What mastery, what learning!	Ma bravo, bravo, bravo!
You amaze me, Don Magnifico. On wines and	Caro il mio Don Magnifico! Di vigne,
Vines and vintages such a discourse	Di vendemmie, e di vino
You've just delivered, I'm lost in admiration.	M'avete fatto una dissertazione.
You're an expert, no question.	Lodo il vostro talento.
(to Ramiro)	
And he's fond of his subject.	Si vede che ha studiato.
(to Don Magnifico)	
Pray go this very moment	Si porti sul momento
To the cellar where my wines are stored and guarded.	Dove sta il nostro vino conservato.
Taste them all, sir. If you can do	Se sta saldo, e intrepido
That and still walk out sober,	Al trigesimo assaggio,
I'll appoint you as steward of my household.	Lo promovo all'onor di cantiniero.
I believe men of talent should be rewarded.	Io distinguo i talenti, e premio il saggio.

Highness, your gen'rous heart gives
As freely as a well. The more one draws
out,
The more there's still to come.

Prence, l'Altezza vostra
È un pozzo di bontà. Più se ne cava,
Più ne resta a cavar.

(to his daughters)

(Daughters, d'you hear him?
He's unable to resist you.
Now I'm to get promotion: that makes it
certain.)
Now my dear little ducklings,
I'll leave you with the king. I'm for the
cellar.

(Figlie! vedete?
Non regge al vostro merto;
N'è la mia promozione indizio certo.)
Clorinduccia, Tisbina,
Tenete allegro il Re. Vado in cantina.

RAMIRO

(to Dandini)

(Observe them both with care, watch all
their behaviour,
And later you shall tell me. Search out
their feelings.
Yes, that's the thing that counts. All
charms and beauty
Fade as the years come on, but the
heart . . .)

(Esamina, disvela, e fedelmente

Tutto mi narrerai. Anch'io fra poco.

Il cor ne tenterò; del volto i vezzi

Svaniscon con l'età. Ma il core . . .)

DANDINI

(to Ramiro)

(As far as these two go,
It's clear enough: hearts cold as pebbles,
And a manner like bullocks.
And as for brains, they've not a thought
to share between them.)
That will be all, then. Be off about your
duty.
And whatever I ordered, do to the letter,
You understand?

Il core
Credo che sia un melon tagliato a fette:
Un torrente l'ingegno,
E il cervello una casa spigionata.

Il mio volere ha forza d'un editto.

Eseguite trottando il cenno mio.
Udiste?

RAMIRO

I do, sir.

Udii.

DANDINI

Go, then, my trusty servant.

Fido vassallo, addio.

Exit Ramiro. Dandini turns to the sisters.

Now at last we're alone here. I'd like to
wager
Your pretty heads are whirling,
And if one asks the reason
The answer lies with Cupid.

Ora sono da voi. Scommetterei

Che siete fatte al torno,
E che il guercietto amore
È stato il tornitore.

CLORINDA

(drawing Dandini to her)

If you please, sir.
I am slightly the elder,
So it's to me, sir,
That you should give your preference.

Con permesso:
La maggiore son io,
Onde la prego
Darmi la preferenza.

Sir, pray allow me,
Look at me, I'm the younger,
I shan't grow up so early.

Con sua licenza:
La minore son io,
Invecchierò più tardi.

CLORINDA

Pardon: she's just a child still.
Look at her awkward manners.

Scusi: quella è fanciulla,
Proprio non sa nulla.

TISBE

Try me . . .

Senta . . .

CLORINDA

I'm yours for ever . . .

Mi favorisca . . .

DANDINI
(breaking away, a little angrily)

Ladies, allow me,
Will you split me in two?
I'll not deceive you.

Anime belle,
Mi volete spaccar?
Non dubitate.

(to Clorinda)

(Trust me, I've got good eyesight and
  I've seen what I wanted.)

(Ho due occhi reali, e non adopro
  occhiali.)

(to Tisbe)

(Pretty one, think of me, you know my
  feelings.
We'll see each other shortly up in the
  ballroom.)

(Fidati pur di me, mio caro oggetto,

Arivederci presto al Spedaletto.)

TISBE

Your Highness is so gracious.

M'inchino a Vostra Altezza.

CLORINDA

I thank you indeed, your Highness.

Anzi all'Altezza Vostra.

TISBE

I'll bring you shortly
Just a little something.

Verrò a portarle
Qualche memoriale.

CLORINDA

Will she!

Lectum.

TISBE

Then to our meeting.

Ce la vedremo.

CLORINDA

What a nerve! But we'll see.

Forse sì, forse no.

TISBE

Mightiest Highness!

Poter del mondo!

CLORINDA

Accept my humble duty.

Le faccio riverenza.

TISBE

I take my leave, sir.

E mi sprofondo.

Exeunt at opposite sides.

The following scene is often moved to the opening of the second act, as in ENO performances, so that the Finale opens with the duet *'Zitto, zitto: piano, piano:'*

Enter Don Magnifico, for whom attendants have brought a richly embroidered cloak. There is a table with writing materials. | *Finale: Chorus and Aria*

CHORUS

He is wonderful to see,	Conciosiacosacchè,
Tasting bottles by the score,	Trenta botti già gustò;
He has drunk enough for three,	E bevuto ha già per tre;
But he still calls out for more.	E finor non barcollò;
He's to run the household here,	È piaciuto a Sua Maestà
By the Prince's new command.	Nominarlo cantinier:
He will guide the royal cheer,	Intendente dei bicchier
With his own baronial hand.	Con estesa autorità,
Cellar door is fastened strong,	Presidente al vendemmiar,
But for him it opens wide.	Reggitor dell'evoè;
So we praise him with a song,	Onde tutti intorno a te
And with merry dance beside.	Ci affolliamo qui a saltar.

DON MAGNIFICO

You confirm it? . . . I'm to stay?	Intendente . . . reggitor?
I'm the steward from today?	Presidente . . . cantinier . . .?
Thank you, thank you. Oh, what joy!	Grazie, grazie . . . che piacer!
What delight at last is mine,	Che girandola . . . ho nel cor.
Lord of spirits, Lord of wine!	Si venga a scrivere
Write it down, ev'ryone,	Quel che dettiamo.
As I desire.	
Six thousand copies	Sei mila copie
I shall require.	Poi ne vogliamo.

They seat themselves around a table, and write.

CHORUS

Now we are ready, sir,	Già pronti a scrivere
Waiting for you.	Tutti siam qui.

DON MAGNIFICO
[17] *(overlooking them)*

'We, Don Magnifico . . .'	Noi Don Magnifico . . .
Put that all in capitals.	Questo in majuscole:
Stupid! In capitals!	Bestie! majuscole!
That's right, like that.	Bravi! cosi.
'We, Don Magnifico,	Noi Don Magnifico,
Duke of this region.	Duca e Barone
He whose magnificent	Dell'antichissimo
Titles are legion:	Montefiascone;
Earl, count and baron,	Grand'intendente;
Lord of the cellar,	Gran presidente,
Butler and chamberlain,	Con gli altri titoli,
Steward etcetera.	Con venti et cetera,
In splendour suitable,	Di nostra propria
This I ordain.	Autorità,
Law indisputable,	Riceva l'ordine,
This shall remain.	Chi leggerà:
Wine is so good a thing,	Di più non mescere
It's not dilutable,	Per anni quindici,
None should put water in,	Nel vino amabile
That's irrefutable.	D'acqua una gocciola,

70

Anyone drinking	Alias capietur
Wine that is watered,	Et stranguletur,
I'll have him	Capietur,
Drawn and quartered,	Stranguletur,
Properly slaughtered.	Perchè et cetera,
Yes, properly slaughtered.	Laonde et cetera,
In witness, etcetera,	Nell'anno et cetera,
I, the etcetera	Barone et cetera
Hereby, etcetera,	Perchè et cetera,
Wherefore, etcetera,	Laonde et cetera,
Dated, etcetera,	Nell'anno et cetera,
Baron, etcetera.'	Barone et cetera.

CHORUS

'Dated, etcetera',	Barone et cetera,
Never a blot.	È fatto già.
'Baron, etcetera',	*(repeat)*
Now that's the lot.	

DON MAGNIFICO

Now post it everywhere,	Ora affiggettelo
All through the town.	Per la città.
Let no teetotaller,	*(repeat)*
Dare pull it down.	

CHORUS

Now let's away, for the	Il pranzo in ordine
Banquet is beckoning.	Andiamo a mettere:
Liquor will flow and	Vino a diluvio
Our troubles will fly.	Si beverà.

DON MAGNIFICO

I'm feeling bountiful,	Premio bellissimo
I'll give a sovereign	Di piastre sedici,
To any man who can	A chi più Malaga
Drink more than I.	Si beverà.

Exeunt, bowing towards Don Magnifico. Enter Dandini and Ramiro, looking cautiously around them. | Duet

RAMIRO [13]

Tell me quickly in a whisper,	Zitto, zitto: piano, piano:
While the others cannot hear us.	Senza strepito, e rumore.
How did those two girls impress you?	Delle due qual'è l'umore?
What reaction did you find?	Esatezza e verità.
Tell me everything you gathered.	*(repeat)*
Tell me what is on your mind.	

DANDINI

Let me tell you *sotto voce*,	Sotto voce a mezzo tuono,
For your private information	In estrema confidenza,
They're a pair of silly boobies,	Sono un misto d'insolenza,
Full of vanity and pride,	Di capriccio, e vanità.
I am only too delighted,	*(repeat)*
They're no longer at my side.	

RAMIRO

Yet my tutor, Alidoro,	E Alidoro mi diceva
Said a daughter of the Baron . . .	Che una figlia del Barone . . .

71

	DANDINI
Oh, Alidoro is a wise one,	Ah! il maestro ha un gran testone;
Or at least pretends to be.	Oca eguale non si dà.

	RAMIRO
Alidoro said a daughter	Alidoro mi diceva
Was the one I ought to marry . . .	Che una figlia del Barone . . .

	DANDINI
Oh, Alidoro is a prize one,	Ah il maestro ha un gran testone;
He's an ass, it seems to me.	Oca eguale non si dà.
(They're two brazen, ogling hussies;	(Son due vere bandverole . . .
If you leave them, you'll be wise).	Ma convien dissimular).

	RAMIRO
But for just a little longer . . .	Se le sposi purchi vuole . . .
We'll go on with our disguise.	Seguitiamo a recitar.

Clorinda runs in from one side, Tisbe from the other.

	CLORINDA
Oh, your Highness, don't forsake me!	Principino, dove siete?

	TISBE
Oh, your Highness, won't you take me?	Principino, dove state?

	CLORINDA, TISBE
Oh, be kind to your beloved.	Ah! perchè mi abbandonate?
Oh, don't leave me in despair.	Mi farete disperar.

	TISBE
I adore you . . .	Io vi voglio . . .

	CLORINDA
I adore you . . .	Vi vogl'io.

	DANDINI
Gracious ladies, wait a moment.	Ma non diamo in bagatelle.
Happy I could be with either,	Maritarsi a due sorelle
But I cannot marry two.	Tutte insieme non si può.
So what shall I say to you?	*(repeat)*
One I'll marry . . .	Una sposo . . .

	CLORINDA
	(impatiently)
And the other?	E l'altra?

	DANDINI
The other . . .	E l' altra . . .
	(pointing to Ramiro)
On my friend I will bèstow.	All'amico la darò.

	CLORINDA, TISBE
No, no, no, no, no,	Nò, nò, nò, nò, nò,
Wed a courtier, oh, no!	È un scudiero! oibò! oibò!

	RAMIRO
	(placing himself between them)
I will be a loving husband.	Sarò docile, amoroso,
I will cherish you for ever.	Tenerissimo di cuore.

CLORINDA, TISBE
(with an air of disdain)

No, a courtier's not for me.	Un scudiero! no, signore.
No, his wife I'll never be.	Un scudiero! questo nò.

CLORINDA

I'll not wed below my station.	Con un'anima plebea!

TISBE

You can see he's rather vulgar.	Con un'aria dozzinale!

RAMIRO

I will love you always . . .	Sarò buono . . . Amoroso . . .

CLORINDA, TISBE
(affectedly)

It's revolting, it's revolting,	Mi fa male, mi fa male
Such a notion makes me ill.	Solamente a immaginar.

RAMIRO, DANDINI
(laughing)

I've seen nothing quite so funny,	La scenetta è originale:
And I think I never will.	Veramente da contar.

CHORUS
(offstage)

Room there, make room there. Prepare the way.	Venga, inoltri, avanzi il piè:
Let there be no more delay.	Anticamera non v'è.

Enter Alidoro.

RAMIRO

Say, what is it, Alidoro?	Sapientissimo Alidoro,

RAMIRO, DANDINI

What's this noise about the place?	Questo strepito cos'è?

ALIDORO

There's a lady just arrived,	Dama incognita quà vien,
With a veil upon her face.	Sopra il volto un velo tien.

CLORINDA, TISBE

Who can this be?	Una dama!

ALIDORO

I don't know.	Signor sì.

CLORINDA, TISBE

What's her name?	Ma chi è?

ALIDORO

She will not say.	Nol palesò.

CLORINDA, TISBE

Is she pretty?	Sarà bella?

ALIDORO

Yes and no.	Sì, e no.

Who is she? Chi sarà?

ALIDORO

No one can tell. Ma non si sà.

CLORINDA

Did she speak? Non parlò?

ALIDORO

No, not a word. Signora no.

TISBE

Tell me why? E qui vien?

ALIDORO

I do not know. Chi sa perchè?

ALL

Tell me why? What now? Heaven knows. Chi sarà? chi è? perchè?
Who is she? Shall we see? Yes, indeed. Non si sà . . . si vedrà.

CLORINDA, TISBE

(Oh, how jealous this lady's making me. (Gelosia già già mi lacera,
I'm afraid to see her here.) Già il cervel più in me non è.)
(repeat) *(repeat)*

ALIDORO

Oh, how jealous this lady's making them, (Gelosia già già le rosica,
They're afraid to see her here. Più il cervel in lor non è.)

RAMIRO

Strange emotion now possesses me. (Un ignoto arcano palpito
Who is this that will appear? Ora m'agita, perchè?)

DANDINI

I'm a magnet, no mistaking it, (Diventato son di zucchero,
Drawing all the ladies here. Quante mosche intorno a me.)

Dandini makes a sign to Alidoro to bring the stranger in. Enter Cinderella, richly dressed and veiled.

CHORUS

Never was one more fair, Ah! se velata ancor
Among all earthly creatures. Dal seno il cor ci hai tolto,
Will she unveil her features? Se svelerai quel volto,
Who can say? Che incanto mai sarà?

CINDERELLA

All is not gold that glitters. Sprezzo quei don che versa
Let no deceiver woo me. [14]Fortuna capricciosa:
My suitor must bring to me M'offra, chi mi vuol sposa,
A heart that's good and kind. Rispetto, amor, bontà.

RAMIRO

Can I mistake that singing (Di quella voce il suono
That melts my heart's defences? Ignoto al cor non scende;
Now rapture fills my senses, Perchè la speme accende?
And hope inspires my mind. Di me maggior mi fa.)

Oh, lady, veiled in beauty,
Delightful and radiant being,
Unveil, that we in seeing,
More beauty yet may find.

Begl'occhi che dal velo
Vibrate un raggio acuto,
Svelatevi un momento
Almeno per civiltà.

CLORINDA

And now we'll see the miracle
You've heard so much about.

(Vedremo il gran miracolo
Di questa rarità.)

TISBE

Contain yourself, it won't be long
Before we find her out!

(repeat)

Cinderella unveils. A moment of surprise, of recognition, of uncertainty.

ALL EXCEPT CINDERELLA

Ah!   Ah!

CLORINDA THEN RAMIRO, THEN CINDERELLA, THEN ALL TOGETHER [15]

I'd like to speak my feelings,
But words will not be found.

Parlar . . . pensar . . . vorrei,
Parlar . . . pensar non so.

To see this sight before me,

Questo è un $\frac{\text{(inganno)}}{\text{(incanto)}}$ o Dei!

I'm rooted to the ground.

Quel volto m'atterrò.

ALIDORO

I'd like to speak my feelings,
But words will not be found.
Already he's enraptured.
My plan is proving sound.

(Parlar . . . pensar . . .vorrei.
Parlar . . . pensar non so.
Amar già la dovrebbe
Il colpo non sbagliò.)

DON MAGNIFICO
(running in)

Your Highness, supper's ready now . . .
So . . . what . . . but . . . she . . . Good
   heavens!
Why, what a strange coincidence!
She's so like Cinderella!

Signor . . . Altezza in tavola
Che, che . . . co . . . sì, che bestia!

Quando si dice i simili!
Non sembra Cenerentola?

TISBE, CLORINDA

At first we thought her so, sir.
But look a little closer . . .
Our Cinders has no figure,
And this one's surely bigger.
But still she is no Venus,
We've no cause to take alarm.

Pareva ancora a noi.
Ma a riguardarla poi . . .
La nostra è goffa e attratta,
Questa è un po' più ben fatta;
Ma poi non è una Venere
Da farci spaventar.

DON MAGNIFICO

Surely the thing's impossible.
She's back at home, no clothes to wear.

Sta quella nella cenere,
Ha stracci sol per abiti.

CINDERELLA

(He can't think what to make of it.)

(Il vecchio guarda, e dubita.)

RAMIRO

(She's spotted me, I'm sure of it.)

(Mi guarda e par che palpiti.)

DANDINI

But don't let's stand here motionless,

Ma non facciam le statue.

When supper now is beckoning.	Patisce l'individuo.
Let's all go in to supper now,	Andiamo presto a tavola,
And later there'll be dancing.	Poi balleremo il Taice,
And then I'll pick the fairest one,	E quindi la bellissima
The choicest one, the rarest one,	*(repeat)*
The loveliest in sight.	Con me s'ha da sposar.

ALL EXCEPT DANDINI

Let's all go in to supper now,	Andiamo, andiamo a tavola,
Then dance through all the night.	Si voli a giubilar.

DANDINI

(What an appetite it gives me,	(Oggi che fo da Principe
Acting as His Highness for a day.	Per quattro vo'mangiar.)
Royal duties still allow me	*(repeat)*
Time to tuck a lot of food away.)	

ALL [16]

In a dream I'm in a garden	Mi par d'esser sognando
And among the trees I wander.	Fra giardini, e fra boschetti,
I can hear the river playing,	I ruscelli susurrando,
And the linnet singing yonder.	Gorgheggiando gli augelletti;
All the scene is so delightful	In un mare di delizie
As I wander free from care.	Fanno l'animo nuotar.
But I fear a storm is brewing,	Ma ho timor che sotto terra
Slow to start, but then progressing,	Piano piano, a poco a poco,
All the atmosphere oppressing.	Si sviluppi un certo fuoco,
Then an earthquake sends us falling	E improvviso a tutti ignoto,
Makes the garden look appalling.	Balzi fuori un terremoto,
Rocks will shiver, houses quiver,	Che crollando . . . strepitando,
Trees will tumble, stones will crumble,	Fracassando . . . sconquassando,
Leaving all the garden bare.	Poi mi venga a risvegliar;
And I tremble lest my vision	E ho paura, che il mio sogno
Thus should fade into the air.	Vada in fumo a dileguar.

END OF ACT ONE

Act Two

Scene One. *A room in Don Ramiro's palace.* | *Recitative, Scena and Aria*

RAMIRO

This lovely unknown lady
Has a curious resemblance to that poor
servant,
The girl I saw this morning.
And now this unknown lady
Haunts my mind like a vision. I think
Dandini
Is in love with her himself.
Here he comes. I'll hide myself and see
what happens.

Ah! questa bella incognita
Con quella somiglianza all'infelice,

Che mi colpì stamane,
Mi và destando in petto
Certa ignota premura . . . Anche
Dandini
Mi sembra innamorato,
Eccoli: udirli or qui potrò celato.

Ramiro hides, as Cinderella runs in, pursued by Dandini.

DANDINI

Ah, not so fast, one moment! Half an
hour
I've been pacing up and down waiting to
see you.

Ma non fuggir per bacco! quattro volte

Mi hai fatto misurar la galleria.

CINDERELLA

I am honoured, your Highness, but
please excuse me.

O mutate linguaggio o vado via.

DANDINI

But why? I bring my devotion,
And you act as if I'd hit you.

Ma che? il parlar d'amore
È forse una stoccata!

CINDERELLA

But if my heart were already given?

Ma s'io d'un altro sono innamorata!

DANDINI

What impudence to say so!

E me lo dici in faccia?

CINDERELLA

Ah, please believe me,
And don't be angry with me
Just because I'm being honest.

Ah! mio signore,
Deh! non andate in collera
Se vi parlo sincero.

DANDINI

Who is he?

Ed ami?

CINDERELLA

Please, sir . . .

Scusi . . .

DANDINI

Who is he?

Ed ami?

CINDERELLA

Sir, 'tis your servant.

Il suo scudiero.

RAMIRO
(coming out of concealment)
She loves me! Can I believe it?

Oh gioia! anima mia!

77

ALIDORO
(showing his satisfaction)

Just as I had planned it.   (Va a meraviglia!)

RAMIRO

What, not even all his fortune   Ma il grado e la ricchezza
Can tempt you any longer?   Non seduce il tuo core?

CINDERELLA

Though riches glitter bright, a loving   Mio fasto è la virtù, ricchezza è amore.
heart is stronger.

RAMIRO

Then you'll give me your promise?   Dunque saresti mia?

CINDERELLA

Slowly, remember   Piano, tu devi
You do not know me.   Pria ricercarmi,
First see if I am worthy,   Conoscermi, vedermi,
And get to know my rank and station.   Esaminar la mia fortuna.

RAMIRO

I take you,   Io teco,
Dearest, now and forever.   Cara, verrò volando.

CINDERELLA

Be silent. Let me leave you. This I   Fermati: non seguirmi, io tel comando.
entreat you.

RAMIRO

Do you dismiss me?   E come dunque?

CINDERELLA
(giving Ramiro a bracelet)

Take this bracelet, you'll recognise me   Tieni, cercami, e alla mia destra
When you find its companion.   Il compagno vedrai;
On that day, if you still love me, I'm   E allor . . . se non ti spiaccio . . .allor
yours for ever.   m'avrai.

Cinderella leaves. A pause.

RAMIRO

Dandini, what's your verdict?   Dandini, che ne dici?

DANDINI

My verdict? Well, it's obvious.   Eh! dico che da Principe
She shows contempt of court; I've been   Sono passato a far da testimonio.
devalued.

RAMIRO

She said, 'If you still love me, I'm yours   E allor . . . se non ti spiaccio . . . allor
for ever'.   m'avrai.
But did she really mean it?   Quai misteri son questi?
(seeing Alidoro)
            Oh, Alidoro   Ah! mio sapiente
You have always advised me. I have a   Venerato maestro. Il cor m'ingombra
heart
That calls to a strange adventure.   Non mai provato amore
What says your wisdom?   Che far degg'io?

78

ALIDORO

Do as your heart commands you.	Quel che consiglia il core.

RAMIRO
(to Dandini)

You shall be Prince no longer. I'm grateful to you,	Principe più non sei: di tante sciocche
But now the joke is over. Come in, attendants!	Si vuoti il mio palazzo. Olà, miei fidi!
Give orders to the coachman. In a few minutes	Sia pronto il nostro cocchio, e fra
I'll set out on my search and find my treasure.	Così potessi aver l'ali dei venti.

[18 a]

Yes, I shall find her, I swear it.	Sì, ritrovarla io giuro.
For love, kind love shall guide me.	Amor, amor mi muove:
And she, once more beside me,	Se fosse in grembo a Giove
Never from me shall part.	Io la ritroverò.
I love but her for ever;	*(repeat)*
To her command I yield my heart.	

(gazing at the bracelet)

This golden bracelet she gave me,	Pegno adorato e caro
How dearly now I prize . . .	Che mi lusinghi almeno
But brighter than all its glitter,	Ah! come al labbro e al seno,
The light that's in her eyes.	Come ti stringerò!

CHORUS

Oh, what a change is on him,	Ah! qual tumulto ha in seno!
It takes us by surprise.	Comprenderlo non so.

RAMIRO, CHORUS [18 b]

In ev'ry dwelling, our purpose telling	Noi voleremo, domanderemo,
We'll go and find her, and then remind her.	Ricercheremo, ritroveremo.
One moment hoping,	Dolce speranza,
Next moment fearing,	Freddo timore,
My brain's excited,	Dentro al $\binom{mio}{suo}$ core
$\binom{My}{His}$ heart's on fire	Stanno a pugnar;
Love only, love only	Amore, amore,
Rules $\binom{my}{his}$ desire.	$\binom{M'ha}{L'ha}$ da guidar.

Exeunt.

ALIDORO

The night is drawing on now,	La notte è omai vicina
That makes my plan still easier.	Col favor delle tenebre
I'll arrange that the Prince's coach breaks down	Rovesciandosi ad arte la carrozza
Just outside the Baron's house. 'Tis perfect.	Presso la casa del Baron, potrei . . .
He will go in for shelter	Son vicini alla meta
And there he will find her.	I desir miei.

Exit Alidoro. Enter Dandini, pacing up and down. | Recitative and Duet

79

Ex-Prince, that's what I am! Shot in a moment	Ma dunque io sono un *ex*? dal tutto al niente
From the top to the bottom.	Precipito in un tratto?
It had to happen, I see that,	Veramente ci ho fatto
But I look pretty silly.	Una bella figura!

Enter Don Magnifico, with an air of urgency.

DON MAGNIFICO

Pardon me if I press you,	Scusi la mia premura . . .
But these two patient creatures	Ma quelle due ragazze
Are mad with expectation. May I ask, sir,	Stan colla febbre adosso. Si potrebbe
Which one of them you've honoured?	Sollecitar la scelta?

DANDINI

It's all been decided.	È fatta, amico.

DON MAGNIFICO

Decided! What do I hear? Tell me, which is it?	È fatta! ah! per pietà! dite, parlate!
Decided! My little rosebuds . . .	È fatta! e i miei germogli . . .
Are then to ripen in your palace?	In queste stanze a vegetar verranno?

DANDINI

I'll tell ev'rybody shortly,	Tutti poi lo sapranno!
But just now it's a secret.	Per ora è un gran segreto.

DON MAGNIFICO

Just tell me which of them.	E quale, e quale?
Is it Clorry? Is it Tizzy?	Clorindina, o Tisbetta?

DANDINI

Baron, please have some patience.	Non abbiate tal fretta!

DON MAGNIFICO

Oh, won't you tell papa?	Lo dica ad un papà.

DANDINI

In confidence . . .	Ma silenzio.

DON MAGNIFICO

Why, certainly! Now inform me.	Sì sa, via dica presto.

DANDINI

Can no one hear us?	Non ci ode alcuno?

DON MAGNIFICO

Nobody	In aria
But the fly that's on the window.	Non si vede una mosca.

DANDINI

First you must hear of	È un certo arcano
A mysterious event.	Che farà sbalordir.

DON MAGNIFICO
(impatiently)

I stand on tiptoe.	Sto sulle spine.

	DANDINI
	(bringing a chair)
Then take a seat, I beg you.	Poniamoci a sedere.

	DON MAGNIFICO
Tell me, for heaven's sake!	Presto per carità.

	DANDINI
You're no stranger	Voi sentirete
To diplomatic matters.	Un caso assai bizzarro.

	DON MAGNIFICO
(He's so diffident,	(Che volesse
You would think I'm the bride.)	Maritarsi con me?

	DANDINI
So I entreat you.	Mi raccomando.

	DON MAGNIFICO
	(with growing impatience)
I'll do just as you say.	Ma si lasci servir.

	DANDINI
This thing I tell you —	Stia sigillato
You won't divulge it to a single person?	Quanto ora udrete dalla bocca mia.

	DON MAGNIFICO
With me a secret is safe as in a strongroom.	Io tengo in corpo una segreteria.

	DANDINI [19]
You'll be staggered, and astounded,	Un segreto d'importanza,
And bewildered, and quite confounded,	Un arcano interessante
When I tell you this surprising piece of news.	Io vi devo palesar:
It's a thing beyond believing,	È una cosa stravagante,
All your mind it will confuse.	Vi farà strasecolar.

	DON MAGNIFICO
With excitement I am seething.	Senza battere le ciglia,
You can see me hardly breathing.	Senza trar nemmeno il fiato,
I am ready, pray address me as you choose.	Io mi pongo ad ascoltar.
I am standing like a statue.	Starò qui petrificato
I'm directly looking at you.	Ogni sillaba a contar.
I am waiting for your news.	Senza manco trarre il fiato.

	DANDINI
For a long time I've been thinking	Uomo saggio e stagionato,
What should be my wife's position.	Sempre meglio ci consiglia;
It's a difficult decision,	Se sposassi una sua figlia,
I'd appreciate your views.	Come mai l'ho da trattar?

	DON MAGNIFICO
(I'm his counsellor already.)	(Consiglier son già stampato).
Since you put the question to me,	Ma che eccesso di clemenza!
My advice I won't refuse.	Mi stia dunque sua Eccellenza . . .
(repeat)	Bestia! . . . Altezza, ad ascoltar.
For your wife's respect and honour,	Abbia sempre pronti in sala

Thirty men should wait upon her,
Forty serving-women fear her,
Fifty cavaliers be near her.
Dukes in dozens, peers in plenty,
And field-marshals up to twenty.
Then a coach and six to ride in,
And some ice cream ev'ry day.

If that's how she's used to living,
It's by no means what I'm giving.
She shall have no one in waiting.
All her wants anticipating.
With the servants she'll be eating,
She'll complain about the heating.
That's the atmosphere I thrive on,
That is how I earn my pay.

Trenta servi in piena gala,
Cento sedici cavalli,
(repeat)
Duchi, conti e marescialli,
A dozzine convitati,
Pranzi sempre coi gelati,
Poi carrozze e sei lacchè.

DANDINI

Vi rispondo senza arcani
Che noi siamo assai lontani;
(repeat)
Io non uso far de' pranzi,
Mangio sempre degli avanzi,
Non m'accosto a gran signori,
Tratto sempre servitori,
Me ne vado sempre a piè.

DON MAGNIFICO

You are joking.

Non corbella?

DANDINI

No, I swear it.

Gliel prometto.

DON MAGNIFICO

But this business?

Questo dunque?

DANDINI

The Prince's orders.

È un romanzetto.

DON MAGNIFICO

I can't believe you.

Questo dunque?

DANDINI

I won't deceive you.
I am not a royal Highness,
And my fortune's strictly minus.
It was just a sort of masquerade,
And the Prince has had enough of it.
Though a counterfeit I made, sir,
I must now resume my trade.
I'm Dandini, just a valet.
Make the bed, sir, brush your overcoat,
Shave and haircut or manicure!

È un romanzetto.
È una burla il principato,
Sono un uomo mascherato;
Ma venuto è il vero Principe,
M'ha strappato alfin la maschera.
Io ritorno . . . al mio mestiere;
(repeat)
Son Dandini il cameriere
Rifar letti, spazzar abiti,
Far la barba, e pettinar.

DON MAGNIFICO

Shave and haircut or manicure!
This is an outrage,
This is appalling.
I've been insulted,
I'm most offended.
I'll see the Prince at once.
I will not stand it.

Far la barba, e pettinar!
Di quest'ingiuria,
Di quest'affronto
(repeat)

Il vero principe
Mi darà conto.

DANDINI

Pray don't upset yourself,
It's been no trouble.
Don't make a fuss of it,
Ev'rything's over.

Oh non s'incomodi,
Non farà niente.
(repeat)

But now get out of here, Now I command it.	Ma parta subito, Immantinente.

DON MAGNIFICO

I will not budge.	Non partirò.

DANDINI

Need I say more?	Lei partirà.

DON MAGNIFICO

I'll have my rights.	Non partirò.

DANDINI

Right through the door.	Lei partirà.

DON MAGNIFICO

Lay off your hand, sir.	Ci rivedremo.

DANDINI

You understand, sir?	Ci rivedremo.

DON MAGNIFICO

I'll make you pay, sir.	Ci parleremo.

DANDINI

Bid you good-day, sir.	Ci parleremo.

DON MAGNIFICO

No servant's hand shall threaten me.	Non partirò. *(etc.)*

DANDINI

I'll be the master, you can see. Shall I assist you, Or will you go?	Lei partirà. *(etc.)* Pronto è il bastone Lei partirà.

DON MAGNIFICO

I will not go. I'll be ridiculous, Now I can see it. Treacherous fate Has trodden me down. Once I was mighty, Now I'm rejected, Just as a wise man, Might have expected. 'Look at him, look at him!' I hear them calling, Shouting and bawling, All through the town.	Non partirò. Tengo nel cerebro Un contrabasso, Che basso basso Frullando và. Da cima a fondo, Poter del mondo! Che scivolata, Che gran cascata! Eccolo, eccolo! Tutti diranno; Mi burleranno Per la città.

DANDINI

Silly old idiot, Now he can see it, Treacherous fate Has trodden him down. Now from this moment, Learn to behave, sir. Better look smarter, Care for a shave, sir?	Povero diavolo! È un gran sconquasso, Che d'alto in basso Piombar lo fa. Vostr'Eccellenza Ah, ah! guardatelo, Se vuol rasoio, Sapone, e pettine,

I'll do your hair, sir,	Saprò arricciarla,
Nails, if you care, sir.	Sbarbificarla.
Here is the silliest	Ah, ah! guardatelo,
Man in the town.	L'allocco è là.

Exeunt. Enter Alidoro, alone. | Recitative

ALIDORO

My design is succeeding. Cupid will help me,	Mi seconda il destino, Amor pietoso
And he's certain to conquer. Even the darkness	Favorisce il disegno. Anche la notte
Now points in my favour.	Procellosa ed oscura
I can control this accident more smoothly.	Rende più natural quest'avventura.
I can hear the coach approaching. But where's Dandini?	La carrozza già è in pronto. Ov'è Dandini?
Oh, yes, he's in the Prince's carriage.	Seco le vuol nel suo viaggio.
Oh, how impatiently the Prince wanted to be going.	Oh come indocile si è fatto e impaziente!
Love will find out a way on any showing.	Che lo pizzica amor segno evidente.

Scene Two. *A hall in Don Magnifico's house. Cinderella is in her usual dress by the fireside. | Canzone*

CINDERELLA [5]

Long ago there lived a king	Una volta c'era un re,
Who grew weary	Che a star solo,
Of a lonely, single life.	Che a star solo s'annoiò;
All around he sought a wife;	Cerca, cerca, ritrovò:
But there were three who claimed the ring. So what then?	Ma il volean sposare in tre, cosa tar
He chose not the rich nor fair,	Sprezzò il fasto, e la beltà,
But the one nobody knew.	E alla fin sceglie per sé
She was modest, she was simple,	L'innocenza, l'innocenza,
She was simple, kind and true.	L'innocenza, e la bontà.
Tra la la la, tra la la la, tra la la la la.	Là là là là, lì lì lì lì, là là là là.

Recitative and Storm

CINDERELLA
(looking at the bracelet)

How very charming!	Quanto sei caro!
And he that possesses that other bracelet,	E quegli cui dato ho il tuo compagno,
Is most charming of all . . . Goodness gracious!	È più caro di te . . . Qual rumore!
Oh, it can't be, it can't be! Yes, they're back here.	Uh che vedo! che ceffi! di ritorno!
I never thought they'd come back until the daylight.	Non credea che tornasse avanti giorno.

She opens the door.

CLORINDA
(pointing at Cinderella)

Exactly as I told you.	Ma! ve l'avevo detto . . .

DON MAGNIFICO	
It's amazing, amazing!	Ma cospetto, cospetto!
You might say one's a perfect portrait made from the other.	Similissime sono affatto affatto.
They're as like as two peas in a pod.	Quella è l'original, questa è il ritratto.
	(to Cinderella)
Done all I told you?	Hai fatto tutto?

CINDERELLA	
Yes, sir.	Tutto.
Pray tell me what's the reason	Perchè quel ceffo brutto
You all stare at me so?	Voi mi fate così?

DON MAGNIFICO	
Because, because . . .	Perchè, perchè . . .
Because we've met a stranger	Per una certa strega
Who looks the same as you.	Che rassomiglia a te . . .

CLORINDA	
I almost want to strike you	Su le tue spalle
For what has happened.	Quasi mi sfogherei.

CINDERELLA	
Surely you are mistaken.	Povere spalle miei!
What have I done to you?	Cosa ci hanno che far?

TISBE	
Oh, did you hear it?	Oh fa mal tempo!
It's getting quite a tempest.	Minaccia un temporale.

It thunders and lightens. A carriage is heard to break down.

DON MAGNIFICO	
I'll give you quite a tempest.	Altro che temporale!
I wish a stroke of lightning	Un fulmine vorrei
Would shrivel up that saucy valet.	Che incenerisse il cameriere.

CINDERELLA	
But tell me	Ma dite:
What really happened.	Cosa è accaduto? avete
Has something suddenly made you angry?	Qualche segreta pena?

DON MAGNIFICO	
(furiously)	
Stupid, get out. Go and prepare some breakfast.	Sciocca, va là; va a preparar la cena.

CINDERELLA	
All right, I'm going. (Certainly it's upset him!	Vado, sì vado. (Ah che cattivo umore!
Ah, but my own beloved, how can I forget him?)	Ah! lo scudiero mio mi sta nel core.)

She leaves. The storm rages outside. Eventually Dandini and Ramiro enter, in their correct clothes. | Recitative and Sextet

DANDINI	
Sir, please excuse me.	Scusate, amico;

But his Highness's carriage has overturned . . .	La carrozza del Principe
	(recognising Don Magnifico)
Oh, good heavens!	Ribaltò . . . ma chi vedo?

DON MAGNIFICO
(taken aback)

What, you again, sir?	Ah! siete voi?
But, tell me, where's the Prince?	Ma il Principe dov'è?

DANDINI
(indicating Ramiro)

D'you recognise him?	Lo conoscete?

DON MAGNIFICO

His attendant! I'm bewildered.	Lo scudiero! Uh guardate!

RAMIRO

Forgive this intrusion,	Signore, perdonate,
It's rather a lengthy story.	Se una combinazione . . .

DON MAGNIFICO

Your Highness, it's no matter, you are welcome.	Che dici? Si figuri, mio padrone!
	(to his daughters)
(Look, there must be a reason why he came.	(Eh! non senza perchè venuto è qua.
I'm sure that one of you two will get him yet.)	La sposa, figlie mie, fra voi sarà.)
Hey, listen, Cinderella,	Ehi! presto, Cenerentola,
Bring us the chair of state in here.	Porta la sedia nobile.

RAMIRO

No, no, don't take the trouble: in a few minutes	No, no: pochi minuti; altra carrozza
They'll fetch another coach.	Pronta ritornerà.

DON MAGNIFICO

Still, pray allow me.	Ma che! gli pare?

CLORINDA

Don't dawdle, Cinderella.	Ti sbriga, Cenerentola.

Cinderella brings a chair of state for Dandini, whom she imagines to be the Prince.

CINDERELLA

I'm here.	Son qui.

DON MAGNIFICO

For his Highness, you stupid, he's standing there.	Dalla al Principe, bestia, eccolo lì.

CINDERELLA

This one? No, it can't be. He's the Prince?	Questo . . . Ah! che vedo! Principe!

She covers her face with her hands and is about to run away.

One moment! Yes! It's the bracelet!   T'arresta. Che! lo smaniglio!
I've found her. My searching is over.   È lei! che gioia è questa!
Have I found you?   Siete voi?

CINDERELLA
(looking at the Prince's clothes)
You, then, are his Highness?   Voi Prence siete?

CLORINDE, TISBE
(astonished)
I'm astounded!   Qual sorpresa!

DANDINI
A lucky breakdown.   Il caso è bello.

DON MAGNIFICO
(wishing to interrupt Ramiro)
But . . .   Ma . . .

RAMIRO
Be silent.   Tacete.

DON MAGNIFICO
I must be crazy. But . . .   Addio cervello. Se . . .

RAMIRO
No more, sir.   Silenzio.

ALL
Strange indeed!   Che sarà!

DANDINI THEN **RAMIRO** THEN **CINDERELLA**, THEN **DON MAGNIFICO**,
THEN **CLORINDA** AND **TISBE**

Here's a plot there's no denying,   [20] Questo è un nodo avviluppato,
Here's a knot that needs untying,   Questo è un gruppo rintrecciato,
It's a puzzle mystifying,   Chi sviluppa più inviluppa,
All my thoughts and senses trying.   Chi più sgruppa, più raggruppa;
Round and round my thoughts are   Ed intanto la mia testa
  flying.
Hope and dread together vying.   Vola vola, e poi s'arresta,
Doubting fills me, wonder thrills me.   Vò tenton per l'aria oscura,
And my head is in a whirl.   In comincio a delirar.

CLORINDA
(to Cinderella, pushing her roughly)
Why, how dare you, you stupid creature?   Donna sciocca, alma di fango,
It's the limit – such presumption!   Cosa cerchi? che pretendi?
Standing here among your betters.   Fra noi gente d'alto rango
Won't you ever learn your place?   L'arrestarsi è incivilta.

DON MAGNIFICO
Brazen hussy, I won't allow it,   Serva audace! e chi t'insegna
Coming here and pushing forward.   Di star qui fra tanti oroi?
Go at once into the kitchen   Va in cucina, serva indegna,
I don't want to see your face.   Non tornar mai più di quà.

RAMIRO
Keep your distance, you bunch of   Alme vili! invan tentate
  schemers,

And respect the one I treasure.
Or I'll let you feel my anger,
You'll be quickly in disgrace.

Insultar colei che adoro.
Alme vili! paventate,
Il mio fulmine cadrà.

DANDINI

Now the comedy is ended
And the tragedy's beginning.
It is just as I intended,
I'm delighted with the case.

Già sapea, che la commedia
Si cangiava al second'atto:
Ecco aperta la tragedia,
Me la godo in verità.

CLORINDA, TISBE

I'm bewildered.

Son di gelo.

DON MAGNIFICO

I've been cheated.

Son di stucco.

DANDINI

I should say that he's defeated.

Diventato è un mamalucco.

CLORINDA, TISBE, DON MAGNIFICO

But a servant . . .

Ma una serva . . .

RAMIRO

Enough, you heard me.
Hold your tongues or you will pay.
Do what I say, or you will pay.

Olà, tacete:
L'ira mia più fren non ha.
(repeat)

CINDERELLA [21]

Ah, my lord, I pray excuse me.
One request you'll not refuse me.
Pay their blindness back with kindness,
And let mercy crown the day.

Ah signor, s'è ver che in petto
Qualche amor per me serbate,
Compatite, perdonate,
E trionfi la bontà.

DANDINI

She is weeping, ah, how gen'rous,
Such compassion to display.

Quelle lagrime mirate:
Qual candore, qual bontà!

DON MAGNIFICO, CLORINDA, TISBE

Oh the hypocrite, just listen!
In the long run she will pay.
(repeat)

Ah! l'ipocrita guardate!
Oh che bile che mi fa!
Oh che rabbia che mi fa!

DON MAGNIFICO

But now let's all be sensible,
I'm sure you'll understand me.

Ma in somma della somme.
Altezza, cosa vuole?

RAMIRO

Well, then, here's news you've not
expected.
This one's the bride I've selected.

Piano: non più parole,

Questa sarà mia sposa.

He takes Cinderella's hand.

CLORINDA

Oh, he's just making fun, that's all.

Ah! ah! dirà per ridere.

TISBE

A trick that he has done, that's all.

(repeat)

CLORINDA, TISBE, DON MAGNIFICO
(to Cinderella)

See what a trick he's playing now.	Non vedi che ti burlano?
Such funny things he's saying now.	*(repeat)*

RAMIRO

I swear it. She shall be mine.	Lo giuro: mia sarà.

DON MAGNIFICO

I thought it was my daughters	Ma fra i rampolli miei,
I rather thought your Highness . . .	Mi par che a creder mio . . .

RAMIRO
(contemptuously)

I don't think they could love me,	Per loro non son io.
They've shown themselves above me.	*(repeat)*
'You see, he's rather vulgar,	Ho l'anima plebea,
A lack of proper breeding!'	Ho l'aria dozzinale.

DANDINI

Now faithful love may have its way.	Alfine sul bracciale,
	Ecco il pallon tornò;
(repeat)	E il giocator maestro
	In aria il ribalzò.

RAMIRO
(to Cinderella)

Come now, I command! Come now, my own one!	Vieni a regnar: vieni, l'impongo.

CINDERELLA

Firstly, my father's blessing,	Su questa mano almeno,
And let me embrace you, sisters.	E prima a questo seno . . .

She tries to kiss Don Magnifico's hand, and to embrace her step-sisters. They energetically repulse her advances.

DON MAGNIFICO

To blazes!	Ti scosta.

CLORINDA, TISBE

And good riddance!	Ti allontana.

RAMIRO

Who could be so ungrateful?	Perfida gente insana!
They will regret it soon.	Io vi farò tremar.
Wait till I show my anger,	*(repeat)*
They'll sing another tune.	

CINDERELLA

Where am I? What is this magic?	Dove son? che incanto è questo?
Oh, how joyful this must make me.	Io felice, o quale evento!
Is it real, or am I dreaming?	È un inganno? ah se mi desto!
And will someone shortly wake me?	Che improvviso cangiamento!
Such a thing is past believing.	Sta in tempesta il mio cervello,
Such a wonder can't be true.	Posso appena respirar.

THE OTHERS

Hear them moan and hear them mutter.	[22] Quello brontola e barbotta,

89

Hear them stammer, hear them stutter.	Questo strepita e s'adira,
Hear them murmur, hear them mumble.	Quello freme, questo fiotta,
Hear them grouse and hear them grumble.	Chi minaccia, chi sospira,
No one but themselves deceiving.	Va a finir, che a'pazzarelli
They behave as children do.	Ci dovranno strascinar.

RAMIRO, DANDINI

Come now, for happiness awaits	Vieni, amor ti guiderà
And love is calling you.	A regnar, a trionfar.

Ramiro leaves with Cinderella, followed by Dandini and Don Magnifico. | Recitative and Aria

TISBE

We've been deceived and cheated!	Dunque noi siam burlate?

CLORINDA

I'm so furious, I can hardly speak calmly.	Dalla rabbia io non vedo più lume.

TISBE

It's quite beyond belief . . . that Cinderella . . .	Mi pare di sognar . . . la Cenerentola . . .

Enter Alidoro.

ALIDORO

. . . Is to be a Princess.	. . . Principessa sarà.

CLORINDA

Who are you?	Chi siete?

ALIDORO

I came among you begging for alms:	Io vi cercai la carità,
You both repulsed me. But, Cinderella,	Voi mi scacciaste. E l'Angiolina, quella
Who saw that I was wretched, and pitied me,	Che non fu sorda ai miseri,
And whom you treated as a beast of burden,	Che voi teneste come vile ancella,
Now shall rise from her kitchen	Fra la cenere, e i cenci,
And reign in royal splendour. Yes, and your father	Or salirà sul trono. Il padre vostro
Will have to raise a tidy fortune,	Le è debitor d'immense somme. Tutta
For it seems he's squandered her dowry.	Si mangiò la sua dote,
It's very likely that this old ruin of a palace	E forse forse questa reliquia di palazzo,
And all this rather faded furniture	Questi non troppo ricchi mobili
Will shortly find themselves put up for auction.	Saranno posti al publico incanto.

TISBE

What will become of us then?	Che fia di noi frattanto?

ALIDORO

Well, make your minds up.	Il bivio è questo.
You can decide on poverty for ever,	O terminar fra la miseria i giorni,
Or you can beg for pardon.	O pure a piè del trono
If you are humble, the Princess may forgive you.	Implorar grazia ed impetrar perdono.

90

In a few minutes, I warn you,	Nel vicin atrio io stesso,
They'll be having the wedding.	Presago dell'evento,
I thought it as well to make all	La festa nuziale ho preparato:
arrangements.	
So, now go in and see her.	Questo, questo è il momento.

CLORINDA

Must I bow to that baggage? Why it's	Abbassarmi con lei? Son disperata!
outrageous!	

*Exit Clorinda.**

ALIDORO

You see the pill is bitter,	La pillola è un po dura:
But you must swallow it.	Ma inghiottir la dovrà;
There's no escape. Have you reached	Non v'è rimedio. E voi cosa pensate?
your decision?	

TISBE

My decision? Seems to me that I've no	Cosa penso? Mi raccomando alla sorte:
option.	
I prefer humble pie to plain starvation.	Se mi umilio alla fin, non vado a morte.

Exit Tisbe.

ALIDORO

Now, at last, all is settled;	Giusto ciel! ti ringrazio!
Justice is done, and my hopes are	I voli miei non han più che sperar.
fulfilled.	
The proud have fallen, and my dear	L'orgoglio è oppresso, sarà felice
pupil	
Can't but be happy. Kind actions have	Il caro alunno. In trono trionfa la bontà:
met their due reward.	
I'm quite contented.	Contento io sono.

Scene Three. *A hall with a throne. Ramiro and Cinderella enter, with Dandini and Courtiers. Don Magnifico stands in a corner, with Clorinda and Tisbe hiding their faces in vexation.* | *Chorus, Scena and Rondò Finale*

CHORUS

Fortune's a wheel that turns and turns,	Della fortuna istabile
Ruling our joy and our sadness.	La revolubil ruota,
Now it has brought our fair Princess	Mentre ne giunge al vertice,
And brought a time of gladness.	Per te s'arresta immota;
Pride now has gone before a fall,	Cadde l'orgoglio in polvere,
And love has found a way.	Trionfa la bontà.

RAMIRO
(rousing Cinderella)

Dearest . . .	Sposa . . .

CINDERELLA
(almost transfixed with joy)

Forgive me,	Signore, perdona,
If happiness still blinds me.	La tenera incertezza
I still hardly know where to turn. Just	Che mi confonde ancor. Poch'anzi,
lately, remember,	il sai,
I was slaving at the fireside,	Fra la cenere immonda . . .

---

* *For the first performance, Agolini composed an aria for Clorinda, 'Sventurata mi credea', at this point.*

91

And now to heaven I find myself transported.	Ed or sul Trono . . . e un serto mi circonda.

DON MAGNIFICO
(kneeling)

Your Highness . . . let me entreat you . . .	Altezza . . . a voi si prostra . . .

CINDERELLA

As a daughter at last now let me greet you.	Nè mai m'udrò chiamar la figlia vostra?

RAMIRO
(indicating the sisters)

And your proud sisters?	Quelle orgogliose . . .

CINDERELLA

Your Highness,	Ah Prence,
One favour you won't refuse.	Io cado ai vostri piè.
All my misfortunes in this hour are forgotten.	Le antiche ingiurie mi svanir dalla mente.
I gain a throne . . . and as a Princess I do my duty.	Sul Trono io salgo, e voglio starvi maggior del Trono;
Now let this be my vengeance — to grant them pardon.	E sarà mia vendetta il lor perdono.

Born to a life that was lonely,	[23a]	Nacqui all'affanno e al pianto,
I knew no moment of pleasure.		Soffrì tacendo il core;
It was through love, love only,		Ma per soave incanto
I found my joy and treasure.		Dell'età mia nel fiore,
Quickly as lightning in a storm,	[23b]	Come un baleno rapido
Love raised me up, and gave me one to be my own.		La sorte mia, la sorte mia cangiò.
Love raised me up to a throne.		*(repeat)*

(to Don Magnifico and her sisters)

No, no, I'll have no weeping.	No, no! tergete il ciglio:
Don't be afraid of me.	Perchè tremar, perchè?
Give me your hands, and let me now embrace you.	A questo sen volate,
Daughter, companion, and sister,	Figlia, sorella, amica,
Daughter, sister, and	Tutto, tutto, tutto,
Companion before you, you see.	Tutto trovate in me.

(embracing her step-sisters)

ALL
(except Cinderella)

She shames us all, so merciful,	M'intenerisce e m'agita,
So ready to forgive.	È un nume agli occhi miei.
Long may you reign and live . . .	Degna del Tron tu sei,
We share your happiness	Ma è poco un Trono a te.
We greet you, our own Princess.	

CINDERELLA

Father, husband, companions, I greet you.	Padre . . . Sposo . . . Amico . . . oh istante!

	[23c]	
Now no longer by the cinders		Non più mesta accanto al fuoco
Shall I sing my plaintive song, no!		Starò sola a gorgheggiar, no!
Like the daylight joy has risen	[23d]	Ah fu un lampo, un sogno, un gioco

On a night so sad and long.

Il mio lungo palpitar.

(repeat)

ALL THE OTHERS AND **CHORUS**

Long the lane that has no turning
Love and kindness can't go wrong.

Tutto cangia a poco a poco
Cessa alfin di sospirar.

THE END

The rondo finale, illustrating some of Cinderella's two octave runs, in Rossini's autograph score. (Accademia Filarmonica, Bologna)

HER

MAJESTY's ✣ THEATRE,

ITALIAN OPERA HOUSE.

THIS EVENING,
THURSDAY, May 17, 1849,

Will be performed Rossini's Opera,

LA CENERENTOLA

Angelina,	Madlle ALBONI.
Clorinda,	Made. GRIMALDI,
Thisbe, -	Madlle S. HOWSON,
Dandini, - -	Sig. BELLETTI,
Don Magnifico, - -	Sig. LABLACHE,
Alidoro, -	Sig. ARNOLDI,
Don Ramiro, -	Sig. CALZOLARI.

After which, a Selection from

FIORITA.

Principal parts by **Madlle C. ROSATI, &c.**

To be followed by the last Act of BELLINI'S Opera

NORMA.

Norma,	Madlle PARODI,
Adalgisa,	Made GIULIANI,
Pollione,	Sig. BORDAS,
Oroveso,	Sig. LABLACHE.

NOTICE!—The Nobility, Gentry, and the Frequenters of the Opera are respectfully cautioned in purchasing the Libretto. They will do well in taking notice of the Printer's Name, as an imposition is practised by the vending of a spurious and incorrect Book. The editions printed by G. STUART, 38, Rupert Street, Haymarket, may be strictly relied upon, as the text is particularly attended to.

Director of the Music, and Conductor, **M. BALFE.**

To conclude with, a New Ballet, in Five Tableaux, entitled

ELECTRA:
Or, the Lost Pleiade.

Electra,	-	Madlle C. GRISI,
Queen of Stars,		Madlle P. STEPHAN.
Edda,	[betrothed to Ehrick]	Madlle M. TAGLINOI.
Ehrick,	[a Hunter, betrothed to Edda]	M. P. TAGLIONI.
Alcyone,	-	Madlle MARRA,
Maia.	-	Madlle TOMMASSINI,

Doors open at 7 o'clock; the Opera to commence at half-past 7.

STUART, Printer, 38, Rupert-street, Haymarket.

A London playbill from 1849 (Theatre Museum)

Bibliography

A selective list of books in English about Rossini

The most recent biography is by Weinstock (*Rossini*, Oxford University Press 1968) but Francis Toye's biography (*Rossini: A study in tragi-comedy*, Heinemann 1934) is eminently readable. Earlier still is the amusing *Rossini and Some Forgotten Nightingales* by G H Johnstone (Lord Derwent) which contains many amusing anecdotes. By far the greatest commentator to write about this subject, however, was Stendhal. His *Life of Rossini* (trans. Richard Coe, Calder & Boyars, 1970) is a classic of musical criticism, overflowing with enthusiasm for the subject and perpetually stimulating.

The full score of the edition made by Alberto Zedda is published by Ricordi & Co.

Discography

All performances are in Italian, and in stereo, but Abbado conducts the score revised by Alberto Zedda.

Conductor	*Fabritiis*	*Abbado*
Company/Orchestra	**Maggio Musicale Fiorentino**	**LSO**
Cenerentola	G. Simionato	T. Berganza
Magnifico	P. Montarsolo	P. Montarsolo
Ramiro	U. Benelli	L. Alva
Dandini	S. Bruscantini	R. Capecchi
Clorinda	D. Carral	M. Guglielmi
Tisbe	M. Truccato Pace	L. Zannini
Alidoro	G. Foiani	U. Trama

UK Disc Number	GOS631 - 3	2709/039
US Disc Number	LON1376	DG2709 039
Excerpts only	SET345	2538 324 (coupled with excerpts from *The Barber of Seville*)

Excerpts

		UK Numbers only	
Number	**Artists**	**Disc Number**	**Tape Number**
overture	NBC SO/Toscanini	AT 108 ★	
	LSO/Gamba	ECS 531	
	Philharmonia/Giulini	SXLP 30143	
	ECO/Asensio	LGD 023	ZCNEL2005 (cassette) Y8NEL2005 (cartridge)
	RPO/Paita	PFS4386	
	Academy of St Martin's/ Marriner	9500 349	
	LSO/Abbado	2530 559	3300 497
	Chicago SO/Reiner	C45020	
Nacqui all'affanno; Non più mesta	M. Horne	SXL 6149	
	T. Berganza	SDD 224	
	F. von Stade	9500 098	7300 571

★ Mono